Our
UNITED STATES
of AMERICA

CATHOLIC SOCIAL STUDIES

Oliver Corrigan

Teacher's Note

This **Student Text** is designed to be completed in 27 weeks, allowing the student nine weeks to devote to studying his own state. The step-by-step, nine-week guide found in the **Student Workbook** guides the student in researching and writing about the history, geography, and culture of his state. Together, the text and workbook of *Our United States of America: Catholic Social Studies* constitute a complete, 36-week program.

Text and Workbook may be purchased from Catholic Heritage Curricula at *www.chcweb.com*. A daily lesson plan for scheduling *Our United States of America: Catholic Social Studies* can be found in *CHC Lesson Plans for Fourth Grade* and *Our United States of America Daily Lesson Plans*, also available at *www.chcweb.com*.

ISBN: 978-0-9883797-3-2

© 2013 Theresa A. Johnson

Cover and Interior Design: RoseMary Johnson

For more information:
Catholic Heritage Curricula
www.chcweb.com

Printed by Sheridan Books, Inc.
Chelsea, Michigan
February 2016
Print code: 381801

Dedication

To the mothers in my life:

Anne, my mother

Nancy, my mother-in-law

Laura, my beloved wife

And most especially

The Blessed Virgin Mary, patroness of the United States —

Mother to the whole world and everyone in it

(Even you!)

About the Author

Oliver Corrigan holds a Master of Science in Secondary Education from the University of Akron. He teaches social studies at Cristo Rey High School in Columbus, Ohio. He lives with his beautiful wife Laura, and their five equally beautiful children: Daniel, Philip, Kathleen, Veronica, and Brigid.

Table of Contents

3—Southern Region ★ 101

4—Western Region ★ 155

Most Holy Trinity, we put the United States of America into the hands of Mary Immaculate in order that she may present the country to you. Through her we wish to thank you for the great resources of this land and for the freedom, which has been its heritage . . .

Mary, Immaculate Virgin, our Mother, Patroness of our land, we praise you and honor you and give our country and ourselves to your sorrowful and Immaculate Heart. O Sorrowful and Immaculate Heart of Mary, pierced by the sword of sorrow prophesied by Simeon, save us from degeneration, disaster and war. Protect us from all harm. . . .   Amen.

From the Act of Consecration of the U.S. to the Immaculate Heart of Mary by Patrick Cardinal O'Boyle, 1959

INTRODUCTION

Do you like mystery stories? Perhaps you have pretended to be a detective, looking for clues. Then you put the clues together and solved a mystery!

A neighbor once went grocery shopping. She hurried home to put one-year-old John Paul down for his nap. After he was safely in bed, the neighbor began going back and forth from car to kitchen to unload sack after sack of groceries.

At last the neighbor had made her last trip to and from the car, and put the last of the groceries away. Suddenly, she realized that she hadn't put away the bananas that she'd bought earlier. In fact, she hadn't seen the bananas since she left the store. Could they have fallen from a sack onto the floor of the car? Where could the bananas have gone?

The neighbor checked the car; she checked the kitchen again. No bananas. Where could the missing bananas have gone? As she puzzled over the mystery, she heard a loud "burp," coming from John Paul's bedroom. (Have you solved the mystery yet?)

The neighbor hurried to her baby's bedroom to find him sitting on his bed, surrounded by empty banana peels. Mystery solved!

What is a mystery? It is simply a story with "missing pieces" or "missing information." Once we have all the pieces, we understand what happened and the mystery is solved!

When we study the past, we become detectives in the "mystery of history." We seek clues that will tell us who did what, and when, and how, and why. These clues help us learn about societies of the past, but also tell us about the society in which we live. The study of societies is called *social studies*, or the study of people's culture, the way they live, work, play, celebrate, and even worship together.

Clues of recent history aren't hard to find, for you and your parents and grandparents are all living history right now! We can see events happen, and talk with people who saw events happen in the not too distant past.

Often people who lived in previous *centuries*, or one hundred years or more before we were born, wrote down events or stories that happened in their society. Since we can read their stories, it is not difficult to solve "mysteries of history" that happened before any of us were born.

Archaeologists

At other times, historical events happened to people and cultures who had no written language. In this case, clues are found through "detective work" done by *archaeologists*, or people who study *ancient* cultures, cultures that existed thousands of years ago. Archaeologists find these clues by digging through the ruins of ancient settlements. By finding objects (what) used by ancient peoples (who), and studying the land where the objects were found, historians (people who study history) can piece together the clues and solve the "history mystery" of those ancient peoples.

In this study of our United States of America, we will look for "who," "what," "where," "when," "why," and "how" clues. Thinking about these clues will help us better understand the people and events that make up the history of this great country, a history of which we are a part.

When we study what happened before, we can think and ask why events happened. We can think how history might have changed if people had lived their lives differently. As followers of Jesus Christ and His Holy Catholic Church, we understand that being obedient to God's laws and seeking His guidance in all things makes a difference in the way we treat others. When we see others as brothers and sisters, made in the image of God just as we are, we will treat our neighbors near and far with more respect.

As you learn about the social studies of our United States, you will learn of its history, geography, and people who built and are building this nation. Some of the people you will meet invented things that made work easier. Others thought of a system of government and laws to keep our country free and safe. Some heroically gave their lives so that others might live in peace, or led countless souls from bitter darkness into God's saving Light. The actions of these people helped create a "better history" by the way they chose to live their lives. With God's help, we can do the same in today's society.

"Settler's Log House," by Cornelius Krieghoff

Background to Our Country's History and Social Studies

Finding Clues to Understanding

Social studies is the study of a people's *culture*. (Culture is what we call the shared beliefs and practices of a group of people, and the ways they live and work together.) Since the history of a people is related to their present-day culture, history and social studies are often studied together. Knowing a little of our country's historical and cultural background will help you understand what you will study. This knowledge will also help you recognize familiar clues, as you read even more about the events and people mentioned in this background.

Very different countries, circumstances, and people have shaped our nation, and

still do today. These people who first came to the Americas from Europe came from different cultures. As they settled in the new land, each group built its own settlement, apart from the others.

In time, problems or conflicts arose among these different groups of people, and between the countries which had formed these new settlements. Problems arose when one settlement wanted something owned by another, or when one group followed a different religious belief than the others. How could these differences be solved? We will soon begin looking for clues to answer these "mysteries of history."

Landing of Columbus in the New World, 1492

Ancient America

The land in which we live today has not always been divided into states such as the one in which you live. In fact, long ago there were no states at all; there was only the beautiful, majestic land that would someday be called the United States of America.

The "mystery" of this land began in ancient times, when there was no written language. The first people who lived in this land were Native Americans, whose **ancestors**, or great-great-great-great grandparents and beyond, probably came here from Asia! So even Native Americans were long-ago explorers and **immigrants**, or people who traveled from another country first to explore, and then to settle, in a new land.

Early Explorers and Early Settlements

Then, in 1492, the Italian explorer Christopher Columbus sailed from Spain to discover this "new land," which was really a very old land already. But Columbus never set foot in what is now the United States! Instead, his three ships—the *Niña,* the *Pinta,* and the *Santa María*—landed in San Salvador, which is an island between North and South America. However, Columbus' discovery led to the discovery of all the Americas, north, south, and central.

In a little more than a century after Columbus' arrival, explorers from many European countries had sailed to North America. These European explorers found a land rich in furs, minerals, fish, and timber—a land that could be settled and farmed.

A French explorer with Native American guides

By 1620, there were Spanish, Dutch (from the Netherlands), French, and English settlements in various parts of what are now the United States. Some of these early settlements grew into **colonies**, or large settlements that were a little like smaller versions of the countries which settled them.

For example, French settlements in our country were filled with French-speaking people who brought their culture, or social and religious practices, with them. They still thought of themselves as French. They followed French customs or practices, and French law. But the French colonies soon began to have disagreements with the English colonies, who had disagreements with the Spanish colonies, and so forth. Why did these disagreements begin, and how could they be solved?

Differing Religious Beliefs at the Beginning of our Nation

At the time of the first English colony, England was no longer a Catholic country. Catholics and others who did not follow the Church of England were **persecuted**, or punished, and were not allowed to practice their Faith freely. Sometimes this persecution meant that Catholics were imprisoned, had their property taken, or were even killed for their Faith. The first English settlers belonged to this Church of England.

Spanish and French settlers were usually Catholic, while Dutch settlers belonged to yet another non-Catholic church. How did these differences in belief cause problems in this new land, and how could the differences be solved?

Challenges to Development

In addition to problems with cultural and religious differences, geography also presented challenges to be overcome. There were no roads to make travel easier for the new settlers. They followed narrow trails across steep, rocky mountains; dangerous rivers; and blistering hot deserts. They traveled on foot, horseback, or bouncing wagons to reach their new homes.

Geography also had, and still has, an effect on a region's **economy**, or the making, buying, and selling of goods that created jobs. Land in some states was good for **agriculture**, or farming. In other states, the soil was so poor that people had to find other ways to feed and support their families. The economy in these states might be based on **natural resources**, or things that were found in the water or soil. Fish are a natural resource that provided fishing jobs for those who lived near the ocean or lakes. In other places, oil, iron, or even gold found in the ground added to a region's economy, providing jobs for people in that area.

Early settlers also made use of ships and small boats for **transportation**, or ways to carry goods and people, up and down coastlines and rivers. But how could settlers easily reach places far from the coast and rivers? The country could not develop and grow if people and goods could not easily be moved from place to place. Transportation, too, was a problem to be overcome.

Challenges of Government

America's first system of **government**, or system of leaders, laws, and rules by which a nation lives, was not at all like it is today. In fact, there were almost as many systems of government as there were colonies. Dutch settlements were governed differently from English settlements, which were governed differently from Spanish settlements.

At first, the tiny English colonies did well under English rule. Time passed and the colonies grew. Children and grandchildren were born to the first settlers who had come from England. These children,

born in America, began to think of themselves as American, not as English.

At the same time, the country of England became even stronger, and grew to become Great Britain. On our shores, Great Britain began to take over settlements that had once belonged to the French and Dutch, until there were thirteen British colonies.

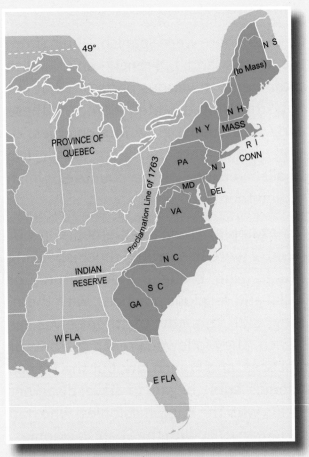

Map of the original 13 colonies

Partly because of goods that were grown or made in the expanding colonies and shipped to England, Great Britain grew wealthier. The British also demanded that people in the colonies pay a certain amount of money, or taxes, to the British government.

But the colonists were not free to make decisions about the country in which they lived. They could not vote to change the British laws that demanded tax money.

Remember that there were no United States yet; there was no American government. There was no United States **Constitution**, or set of rules and laws that were just for Americans. The American colonies belonged to the British, and colonists had to live under British rules, or laws, whether they liked the laws or not. In time, British soldiers were sent to the colonies to make sure the Americans followed the hated British rules.

Who caused these problems with government, and how could the problems be solved? How would decisions made long ago in history benefit the society in which we live today?

Problems with Slavery in the Colonies

As Catholics and Americans, we believe that we should have the freedom to make moral, or godly, choices about the way we live our lives. People who enjoy this freedom can choose where they will live, where they will go to school, where they will work, and how they will worship. As one nation, under God, we are a free people.

But not everyone in the world enjoys such freedoms. It is a sad fact that, even today, some live in **slavery**. People who are enslaved cannot make choices about how to live their lives, how and where they will work, where they will live, go to school, and worship. In fact, a slave is actually owned by another person, who considers the slave to be a piece of his property! The slave owner makes all the decisions about the slave's life. The slave

"The First Slave Auction at New Amsterdam in 1655" by Howard Pyle

7

owner can even sell the slave to another person. Slave owners have even sold fathers or mothers or children to others who lived far, far away. These families were broken up forever, never to see their other family members again.

Jesus Christ took on flesh and became man to be Savior of *all*. We are *all* brothers and sisters, equally valued and loved by our Heavenly Father. We can see from this that slavery is an evil, because it treats some people as more valuable than others. Because of this, our country has laws that forbid slavery. But it was not always this way.

For thousands of years, people who lived in Africa, the Middle East, and Europe either bought and sold, or owned, slaves. Many Native American tribes also owned slaves.

At its very beginnings, slavery was legal in America, too, although not very many people owned slaves. After a time, Americans began to see that slavery was a moral evil. Some states began to outlaw slavery, or make it illegal.

In other states, slavery was still legal. People who were for slavery, and people who were against slavery, both felt very strongly that their beliefs were right!

As the number of states grew from the original thirteen, "free" states that were against slavery wanted any new states to be "free" states, too. But slave states did not want to be outnumbered by free states; they wanted new states to be slave states. When a new state was settled and asked to become part of the United States, you can imagine the fights that broke out!

How would this argument between good and evil be solved? Who would lead the fight to end the terrible evil of slavery?

Of course, all of these historical questions arise because of events that happened in individual states across this vast country of ours, states like the one in which you live.

"Bringing in the Cotton" by William Aiken Walker

"Battle of Spottsylvania" by Thure de Thulstrup

What part did your state, and the people of your state, play in our history? How did their actions change the society in which you live today?

This social studies book will give you a taste of your state's part, but when you finish this text, you will see that there is so much more to discover! The workbook that accompanies this text continues your historical studies for the last nine weeks of the school year. During these nine weeks, you will experience a completely new, hands-on understanding of your own state.

Conclusion

As you begin this text, be on the lookout for "who, what, when, where, and why clues," clues to the "mystery of history" of our land. These clues, the "evidence" that you find, will help you understand how the land and people who lived here formed the country that we know today: our United States of America.

Student Workbook: Complete pgs. 1-4.

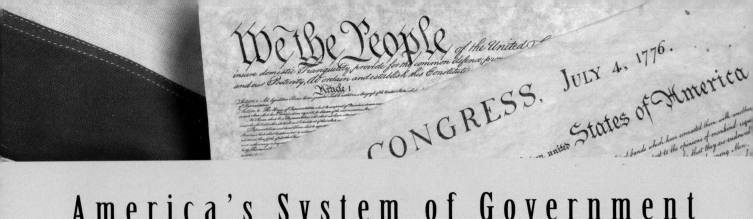

America's System of Government

To help us understand what we will soon learn about our nation, we first need to understand that our United States has a history that is very different from the rest of the countries in the world. Most countries that existed before America were ruled, or *governed*, by kings or emperors that were not chosen by the people they ruled. This system of *government*—the way a country is ruled—was only as good as the king or emperor. If the king was a bad and cruel king, the people suffered terribly, and there was nothing they could do about it. They could not choose, or vote in, a new king. So, the people suffered.

Before 1776, America was not its own country. America was a collection of thirteen *colonies*. (A *colony* is a land that doesn't "belong" to itself, but to another country.) America belonged to Great Britain. Great Britain made the rules for America, and many of the rules made American *colonists*—the people who lived in the colonies—very unhappy.

The British made Americans pay taxes on goods like tea, and more taxes when they did business. Americans couldn't always say what they thought, or meet in public, without fear of being arrested by the British. Americans even had to make room in their houses for British soldiers to live with them. Imagine if you had to give up your bedroom, because soldiers moved into your house whether you wanted them there or not!

The Americans did not like these rules, but there was nothing they could do. Sometimes British soldiers harmed Americans, but instead of being put in jail, nothing was done to punish them. The Americans didn't think this was at all fair!

Then, in 1775, the thirteen American colonies decided that they had had enough. America *revolted*, or refused to let Great Britain tell them what to do anymore. This revolt turned into the American Revolution, or the *Revolutionary War*. Great men and women worked and fought together to build a new nation, "conceived in liberty," founded in freedom.

A *Declaration of Independence* was written to tell the British that from now on, America would be free of their rule. (Every American should read the Declaration, for it reminds us that our most important rights don't come from government, but from God.) On July 4th, 1776, this Declaration was signed. We now celebrate this day of freedom every year as *Independence Day*.

The colonies fought against Great Britain, and won their independence, their freedom, to become their own country and make their own rules or laws. Americans knew that they did not want a king or an emperor. They wanted to be able to *vote* for, or choose, their leaders. They wanted to be able to make good laws, and vote on those laws.

After the war, American leaders met together to write a set of laws that would be fair for everyone. This set of laws was and is called the *Constitution of the United States*. The Constitution is the law of our land.

The Constitution set up a form of government that was divided into three parts, or branches: the executive, the legislative, and the judicial.

The *executive* branch is led by the president, who is *elected*, or voted for, by the people.

The *legislative* branch is called *Congress*. Congress is made up of the *House of Representatives*, and the *Senate*. The people in Congress are *elected*, or voted for, by the people. Members of Congress *represent*, or speak for, the people who elect them.

Imagine if 1,000 people from Alaska wanted a law made or changed. Think of how far they would have to go, to drive or fly all the way to our nation's capital in Washington, D.C., to let the government know they wanted a different law! Because we have representative government, the people of Alaska—and all the other states, too—don't have to travel all the way to the nation's capital to speak up. Instead, they can tell their representatives in Congress what they want changed, and their representatives and senators will vote to make the changes that people want.

The *judicial* branch of government is made up of the judges of the Supreme Court. When there is disagreement about a law, this Court decides whether or not the law agrees with the Constitution, the main law of our great land. (All laws must agree with the Constitution.)

This new system became the *federal* government, or government of our whole nation. This system worked so well that a very similar type of representative government is also used in each of the states. Citizens vote for people who will represent them in the federal, or national, government in Washington, D.C. But citizens also vote for people who will represent them in their own states. (In some states, these representatives are called *delegates*. But whether they

are called representatives or delegates, they are chosen to represent, or speak for, the people who voted for them.)

Because Americans wanted to participate in their own government, to be part of making fair rules and fair laws, they fought for the liberty to form a new kind of government. Americans looked back at other governments in the history of the world and learned from the achievements and mistakes of other nations. Many of the ideas for America's government were taken from ancient Greece, from ancient Rome, and even from England itself. (Yes, even though the Americans were fighting for freedom against England, there were many things about England that they still liked.)

In the end, the Founders designed a new kind of government that had never existed before in the whole world. This system of government is found in the Constitution of the United States, the law of our land. Whether you live in the Southern States, Midwestern States, Western States, or Northeastern States, the people of your state, too, must follow the laws found in our nation's Constitution. How different our lives are today, because of brave men and women who shaped our history!

"We hold these truths to be self-evident, that all men are created equal, that they are endowed by their Creator with certain unalienable Rights, that among these are Life, Liberty, and the pursuit of Happiness."

—from the *Declaration of Independence*

Student Workbook: Complete pgs. 5-6.

"Declaration of Independence" by John Trumbull

Canada

Lake
Winnipeg

Ontario

Lake
Nipigon

Quebec

St Lawrence R.

New Brunswick

Lake Superior

MINNESOTA

MAINE

WISCONSIN

Lake
Michigan

VERMONT

★ Augusta

Montpelier

Lake
Huron

Concord

NEW HAMPSHIRE

Saint Paul ★

Albany

★ **NEW HAMPSHIRE**

Boston

Madison ★

MICHIGAN

Lake Ontario

★

MASSACHUSETTS

IOWA

Lansing ★

Hartford ★

Providence

RHODE ISLAND

Lake Erie

NEW YORK

CONNECTICUT

es Moines ★

PENNSYLVANIA

NEW JERSEY

Missouri R.

Springfield ★

INDIANA

OHIO

Harrisburg

Trenton ★

Indianapolis

Columbus

Dover ★

★

Annapolis

DELAWARE

ILLINOIS

Ohio R.

Washington D.C.

★

MARYLAND

Charleston ★

Missouri R.

WEST VIRGINIA

Richmond

Jefferson
City ★

Frankfort

VIRGINIA

Ohio R.

MISSOURI

KENTUCKY

Raleigh

★

Nashville ★

ARKANSAS

NORTH CAROLINA

TENNESSEE

Little Rock ★

Columbia

★

Atlanta

SOUTH CAROLINA

★

*Atlantic
Ocean*

MISSISSIPPI

GEORGIA

Montgomery

★

LOUISIANA

Jackson ★

ALABAMA

Baton Rouge ★

★ Tallahassee

FLORIDA

Gulf of Mexico

The United States of America

**Bahama
Islands**

0	125 Miles	250 Miles	500 Miles

0	125 KM	250 KM	500 KM

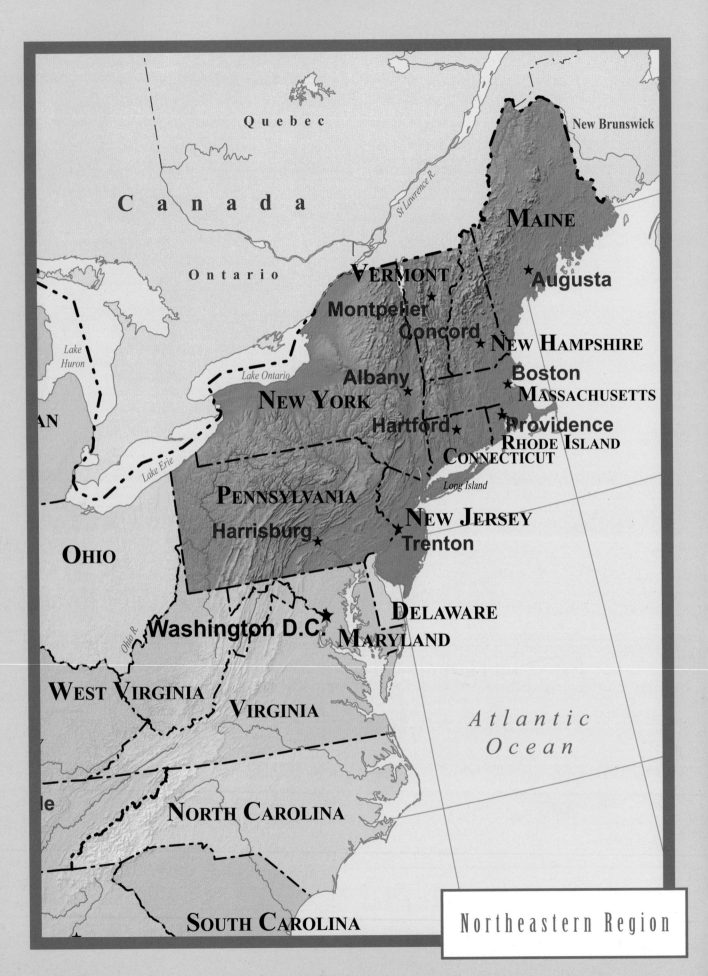

Quebec

New Brunswick

C a n a d a

O n t a r i o

St. Lawrence R.

MAINE

Lake Huron

Lake Ontario

VERMONT
Montpelier

★Augusta

Concord
★

NEW HAMPSHIRE

Albany
★

Boston
MASSACHUSETTS

NEW YORK

Hartford
★

Providence
RHODE ISLAND

Lake Erie

CONNECTICUT

Long Island

AN

PENNSYLVANIA

NEW JERSEY
★

Harrisburg
★

Trenton

OHIO

Ohio R.

Washington D.C.
★

DELAWARE

MARYLAND

WEST VIRGINIA

VIRGINIA

Atlantic Ocean

le

NORTH CAROLINA

SOUTH CAROLINA

Northeastern Region

14

The Battle of Long Island, New York, 1776

Connecticut · Maine · Massachusetts · New Hampshire · Rhode Island

The Northeastern Region

Vermont · New York · Pennsylvania · New Jersey

Part 1

The Northeastern Region

There is nowhere else on earth where you can see evidence of God's powerful hand of creation quite like in the northeastern United States. The mighty forests of the Appalachian Mountains pierce through the region and beyond. Rolling rivers from the mountains flow down into the majestic Atlantic Ocean.

Crossing the Atlantic from Europe, the first European settlers arrived in 1620, and since then *immigrants*—those who leave their home country and come to settle in a new land—have never stopped coming. From the very beginning, these immigrants have made the Northeast the center of American business.

Today, the Northeast region has the most crowded *population*, or number of people who live in an area. One in five Americans live in the "megalopolis"—an interconnected series of suburbs and cities from Boston to Washington, D.C. From some of the biggest cities in the country, to family farms, to mighty forests and mountains, God's natural beauty shines through.

The Northeast Region is divided into two smaller regions—the New England region and the Mid-Atlantic region.

NEW ENGLAND REGION

The New England states are: **Connecticut, Maine, Massachusetts, New Hampshire, Rhode Island**, and **Vermont.**

All the U.S. regions are named for their location except New England. In the early years of settlement, conflict with Native Americans and the French eventually led to complete English control of the area. This "New England" thus had a *unique* or one-of-a-kind culture and identity. Like all *cultures*—the shared customs, beliefs, and practices of a group of people and the ways they live and work together—New England's culture is hard to define.

Originally settled mostly by strict **Puritans**, New England has also always been a leader in new ideas. It was New England that started protesting poor treatment from "Old" England in a series of events that would lead to the American Revolution and the birth of a new nation—the United States.

Visitors and residents alike find that spring in New England can be very rainy and cloudy. Summers can get pretty hot, but as you move farther north the weather becomes milder. But when many people think of New England, they think of autumn. The season starts a little earlier than in most places, so the "you have to see them to believe it" bright colors of the autumn leaves are the only excuse you need to visit. Then, once the leaves are gone, prepare for a snowy winter. Mountain and ski resorts make good use of the more than 98 inches of snow that drop each year.

Turn to **LESSONS ALIVE!** on pg. 7 of your workbook for enrichment activities.

Connecticut
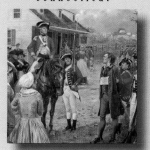

Maine

Massachusetts

New Hampshire

Rhode Island

Vermont

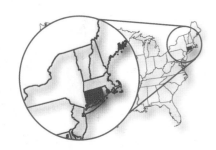

Connecticut

Hartford

Do you have to be big to be important? Of course not! If you need proof, just look to Connecticut. Our third smallest state (Which are the smallest?*) has made a huge impact. In fact, without this tiny state our country might not even exist today. Read on to find out why.

Connecticut was one of the earliest places in the United States to be settled by Europeans. From the very beginning, the settlers of this little British colony did things differently. In 1639, they created the first written rules for government in what would become the United States. These rules were called **The Fundamental Orders**, and declared that Connecticut would be governed (ruled) by "the free consent (permission) of the people." Some people consider these orders to be the world's first written **constitution**, or set of laws that rule a land.

Over a century later, some of the most famous **patriots**—people who love their country so much that they are willing to fight and die for it—in the American Revolution came from Connecticut. Before being captured and hanged by British soldiers,

patriot **Nathan Hale** declared "I only regret that I have but one life to give for my country."

Meanwhile, **Benedict Arnold**—up to that time one of America's greatest Revolutionary War generals—secretly switched sides. He betrayed his troops, joining the British side to fight against those who had been his friends! Even today, to call someone a "Benedict Arnold" is to call him a horrible **traitor**, or one who betrays a friendship or a country.

One of these men from Connecticut stood up for his beliefs and died for it. The other betrayed his beliefs and lived the rest of his life in comfort. Who do you think made the right choice?

Patriot Nathan Hale, by Don Troiani

*Answer: Delaware and Rhode Island

18

After the Thirteen Colonies won their independence from Great Britain, their problems were not over. Now, the new states began to argue amongst themselves! Less populous states, or states with fewer people, were afraid that states with more people would have more power. More populous states thought the opposite would happen. What an argument! How could this difference of opinion ever be solved to everyone's satisfaction?

Members of Congress in the House of Representatives

The first prayer in the First Continental Congress, 1774

While writing the **Constitution**, delegates from Connecticut came up with a solution: **Congress** (the government body that makes federal laws) would consist of two houses (groups) called the **Senate** and the **House of Representatives**. In the Senate, all states would have the same number of representatives—this made the less populous states happy. In the **House of Representatives**, the number of representatives would be based on how many people lived in the state—this made the more populous states happy. Called "**The Great Compromise**," this is the way our government still works today. And we have Connecticut to thank for it!

Connecticut lies on the northeastern seaboard between New York to the west and south, Massachusetts to the north, and Rhode Island to the east. The earliest inhabitants of this land were Native American Algonquian. The Algonquian called the land Quinnechtukgut, which means "Beside the long tidal river."

This long river truly is long—in fact, the Connecticut River is the longest river in New England. The river flows south through New Hampshire, Vermont, Massachusetts and Connecticut before emptying into the Long Island Sound. (A **sound** is a long, broad inlet of the ocean.) On the southern boundary of Connecticut, this beautiful sound separates the state from Long Island, New York.

Captain Kidd, by Howard Pyle

equipment. In fact, so many helicopters and airplanes are built here that Connecticut even has an official state aircraft—the F4U Corsair.

The *Turtle*, the world's first submarine, was built in Connecticut, and the world's first nuclear submarine, the *USS Nautilus*, is still on display in the city of Groton. Not surprisingly, Connecticut is a world leader in manufacturing submarines. Other industries manufacture heavy machinery, chemicals, medicines, and scientific instruments.

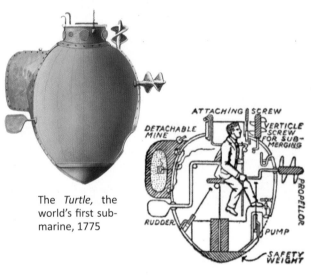

The *Turtle,* the world's first submarine, 1775

In the Long Island Sound are the tiny Thimble Islands. If you wanted to visit one of them every day it would take you a whole year to see them all. (Do you know how many islands there are?*) Legend says the pirate Captain Kidd buried his stolen treasure on one of these islands. Would you like to visit and see if you can find it?

Easy water access quickly turned Connecticut into an important **industrial** state, a state where people make their living in factories. These factories were built up on the shores of the Connecticut River, so that goods could be shipped easily to stores and homes all over New England.

Today, Connecticut is still a major manufacturing state. It is best known for its production of transportation

Hartford, the capital city, is one of the biggest centers for the insurance industry. Farmers provide dairy and poultry products, while fishermen catch lobster. Since the southern part of the state is so close to New York City, many people live in Connecticut but travel to work across the state line. At the same time, millions of visitors around the country come to Connecticut each year to play on the beaches or relax in historic colonial towns.

Answer: 365 days in a year = 365 islands

Have you ever wondered at the beautiful variety of people and customs and cultures that make up America? Visit a large city, and you can find Vietnamese, Chinese, French, Middle Eastern, Mexican restaurants and more. Why is this?

The United States is a nation of immigrants, or people who have come from another land to live here. The first immigrants were Native Americans, who arrived from Asia long, long ago.

Explorers from other lands may have visited our shores long ago, but people from Spain were the first to settle, or stay to build communities. After the Spanish came settlers from England, France, and Holland (the Netherlands). These settlers from Europe sometimes brought with them servants and slaves; some of these were from Africa.

In time, immigrants came to America from Ireland, Italy, Poland, Russia, China, Japan, Vietnam, Cuba, Nigeria, Ethiopia, Somalia, Iran, and the Holy Land (Israel) . . . until our day, when the United States now is made up of people who have come from every place in the world!

Why did these immigrants come? Most came to build better lives; some were rich, but most we would consider poor. They may have suffered hunger, wars, or bad governments in their countries, and desired the freedoms of religion and speech that we enjoy in our nation.

These immigrants from every country came together to live and work as one people: Americans.

Are you an immigrant, or a child or grandchild of immigrants? Then you, too, are part of this "Mystery of History." Would you like to do a little "detective work" to find out? Ask your parents or grandparents!

Student Workbook: Complete pgs. 8-9.

Immigrants on the deck of an ocean steamer passing the Statue of Liberty, 1887

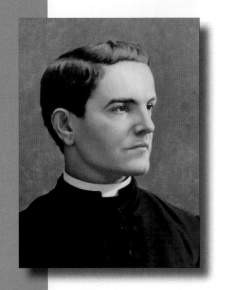

Connecticut's
Catholic Heritage

The Story of Fr. Michael McGivney

With a heavy heart, **Michael J. McGivney** decided to give up his dream of becoming a priest. He had just received word that his father had died, so he quickly left his seminary in Montreal, Canada and returned to his hometown of Waterbury, Connecticut. His father had worked a difficult job in a brass factory, but now that he was dead his family would have no income, no money to live on. Rather than let the family starve, young Michael knew he had to return home, get a job, and help his mother raise his brothers and sisters. If he didn't, who would?

Why wouldn't anyone help them? The year was 1873, and the McGivney family had a problem: they were Catholics. At this time, many non-Catholics feared and distrusted Catholics. Catholics were usually forced to take the most dangerous jobs with the lowest pay, yet often they were not allowed to be part of organizations that might help them. Also, insurance companies refused to sell to Catholics. That meant that when a Catholic worker died, his family was left with no money to survive.

A group of kind priests saw in Michael a true calling to the priesthood and eventually helped him return to seminary closer to his family. He was finally ordained and said his first Mass in his hometown. His mother and brothers and sisters were all proudly in attendance.

Fr. McGivney began his priestly ministry on Christmas Day, 1877, at St. Mary's Church in New Haven, Connecticut. Christmas should be a day of brotherhood among men, but again Father Michael faced **prejudice**, or unkindness toward him because he was Catholic. St. Mary's was New Haven's first Catholic Church and the newspapers complained about how the building "blemished," or somehow made their nice neighborhood ugly.

Despite this prejudice, Father Michael went about his duties with compassion. One night, an angry young man got drunk and then shot and killed a police officer. The young man was sentenced to hang. He was hated by the town, but Father Michael showed kindness to the young man. Every day, he comforted him in jail.

On the day of the execution, it was Father Michael who started crying. The jailed young man—now filled with the love of Christ that the kind priest had shown him—comforted Father Michael and then went peacefully to his death. After this, Father Michael spent the rest of his life helping people who struggle to stop drinking. Today we know this can be an addictive condition called alcoholism, which is overcome only through God's grace and heroic personal effort.

Father Michael spent a long time praying about the problems Catholics were facing in the United States. He started talking to his parishioners about creating an organization to help Catholic men strengthen their faith and provide money for their families if they were to become sick or die.

It was in a small church basement that this new group held their first meeting. All it needed was a name. Someone suggested the Knights of Columbus. The word "Knights" made people think of *chivalry*, the noble honor of fighting for a good cause. The name "Columbus" referred to Christopher Columbus, the Catholic discoverer of the New World. This was a reminder that Catholics have

played an important role in American history from the very beginning. Catholics were not to be feared or distrusted. (Sometimes people fear what they don't understand.) The Knights worked hard to explain to non-Catholics about our beliefs. Non-Catholics and Catholics both discovered we have much in common and we should try to understand each other's differences.

That small group in a basement soon grew to become the world's largest Catholic fraternal (male friendship) organization. Their insurance program is now one of the most successful in the world.

Today, the Knights have more than 15,000 councils in 13 countries. Nearly 1.8 million Knights donate $150 million, and 70 million volunteer hours each year. They created the first nationwide

"Fr. Michael J. McGivney" by Antonella Cappuccio

Knights of Columbus

blood donor program in history, and especially work to help people with physical and mental disabilities. The Knights are primarily responsible for Columbus Day becoming a national holiday and adding the phrase "under God" to the Pledge of Allegiance.

The world has changed a lot since Father Michael's time, but following the ideas of charity, unity, fraternity, and patriotism, the Knights of Columbus continues his mission into the 21st century.

Did You Know? The French and Indian War

After Christopher Columbus discovered this new land called America, many European countries wanted to explore this land and start settlements here. These countries included Spain, France, England (or Great Britain), and Holland (the Netherlands). With all these countries interested in the same region, it wasn't long before they started to fight over it.

Soon, the French and British went to battle over the same land. In the 1750s, some Native American tribes joined the French to fight against the British. At first, the French and Native Americans were able to chase the British away from land that they both wanted. But within a few years, the British **defeated**, or beat, the French. Now the British owned most of the land that France had claimed.

Interestingly, Canada was also owned partly by the British and partly by the French. Because of their history, most Canadians now live in English-speaking regions, or **provinces**. But in the Canadian province of Quebec, which was first colonized by the French, the citizens still speak French. How do you think our society might be different today if the British had not won the French and Indian War so long ago?

Student Workbook: Complete pgs. 10-13.

Augusta

Maine

Vikings, adventurous warrior-sailors from northern Europe, may have sailed their Viking ships across the Atlantic to Maine in the year 1000 A.D.—almost 500 years before Columbus! Of course, Columbus didn't know that and neither did anyone else until very recently. Just when we think we know everything, historians always discover something new. It's a "mystery of history" that you've just discovered, too!

Since nobody knew about the Vikings, Maine was discovered—again—by English explorer **John Cabot** in 1498. Yet it would be another hundred years before Europeans would try to settle there. The French built the first settlement in 1604, but it wasn't long before a number of English settlements popped up along New England's coast.

These English settlements had a lot of problems, but in 1677 they were made a part of the **Massachusetts Bay Colony**, about which you will soon hear more. The French gave up their **territory**, or land that they claimed as their own, in 1763, after the **French and Indian War**. Yet, many of the French settlers stayed on.

Today, one-third of Maine's population is of French descent and 7% speak French as a first language! Algonquian-speaking Native American tribes lived in Maine for thousands of years, but lost most of their land in unfair **treaties**. (A **treaty** is an agreement between two groups who are arguing or at war over who owns a piece of land.) Yet, Maine's Penobscot River and Penobscot Bay are named in honor of an Algonquian tribe.

Viking explorer Leif Ericsson discovers America, by Christian Krohg

25

Portland Head Light lighthouse

After the American Revolution, Maine remained a part of Massachusetts, even though, as you can see on a map, the two states are not even connected! As Maine's population grew, many people wanted it to be its own state. Eventually, Mainers got their wish and became the 23rd state in 1820.

Maine sits on the northeastern corner of the country, farther east than any other state. Because of this, the people in West Quoddy Head, the easternmost part of Maine, get a special treat each day. They can watch the sun rise before anyone else in the country. (Why?*)

Maine borders the Canadian **provinces** of New Brunswick and Quebec. (A **province** is like a state, a section of land that is part of a larger country.) Maine also borders New Hampshire, making Maine the only state bordered by just one other state. Maine is most famous for its southern border, a 3,478 mile-long rocky coastline on the Atlantic Ocean.

Over 1,100 islands of every size lie along this state's shore. Mount Desert Island and some smaller islands make up Acadia National Park, the only national park in the northeastern United States. Mount Desert Island is home to Cadillac Mountain, the highest mountain peak along the entire Atlantic coast of North America.

Because many ships were wrecked trying to travel between these islands and along rocky shores, President Washington in 1790 had the Portland Head Light lighthouse built to help ships safely navigate, or travel, these waters. As one of the oldest and most famous lighthouses in the country, it—and 70 others like it—attracts many tourists to Maine.

Maine is so big you could almost fit the other five New England states inside of it. However, most people in Maine live only 25 miles from its rocky coast. This is because the other two-thirds of Maine consists of beautiful wilderness with thick forests and glistening lakes, where very few people live. But people do love to visit this area to camp and fish.

The mighty Appalachian Mountains run southwest across the state. (In Maine these mountains are officially named the "Henry Wadsworth Longfellow

*Answer: The sun rises in the east.

Mountains," in honor of Maine's most famous poet.) The Appalachian Trail starts at Mount Katahdin in Baxter State Park. Some people make it their life's ambition to hike the trail's 2,181 miles all the way to trail's end at Springer Mountain, Georgia. Are you up for the challenging hike?

For a long time, shipbuilding was Maine's most important industry. In early American history, Maine's tall, white pines were a natural resource and just what shipbuilders needed to make the tall masts of sailing ships. You can still hire "schooners" like these to take an old-time sailing adventure.

Today, most of the Pine Tree State's pine trees have been replaced by oaks and maples. Yet the making of wood products, like paper, is still Maine's most important industry. In fact, the Strong Wood Products factory makes more than 20 million toothpicks a day!

Do you eat fish and other seafood on Friday? Maybe part of your dinner came from Maine, whose seafood is loved the world over. Almost 90% of the country's lobster comes from this state. Most of Maine's land is not good for growing crops, but the best soils grow potatoes, and Maine harvests more wild blueberries than anywhere else in the world. Other industries include shoe-making, electrical equipment, machinery, textiles (clothing), food processing, medical technology, and tourism.

Milton Bradley of Vienna, Maine, launched the board game industry so you can always have fun on a cold, rainy day. When the weather clears and you go outside, don't forget your earmuffs. They were invented by a Maine teenager!

Pushing a lobster trap into the water

Victory Chimes, the only remaining three-masted schooner on the East Coast

Maine's Catholic Heritage

The Story of Fr. Sebastien Rale

When Europeans discovered the Americas, many saw these new lands as an opportunity for wealth and a chance to take more property for themselves. Before long, the nations of Europe were fighting each other over who could own this valuable new continent. Most Europeans ignored the fact that there were already people living here—millions of Native Americans within dozens of different tribes. Because they looked and acted in ways that seemed strange to the Europeans, many settlers considered Native Americans "savages" and saw them as little more than animals. Thankfully, not everyone felt this way. One of these was **Father Sebastien Rale**. He saw Native Americans as they really are—people like himself.

The young French priest sailed to New France (now Canada) in 1689, to spread the Faith to the native people. He worked in various missions in New France before being assigned to a small village called Norridgewock along the Kennebec River in Maine. It was here that he ministered to the Abenaki tribe for the rest of his days. He enriched their new Catholic Faith, and they enriched his whole life.

Father Rale believed Abenakis should be treated with the same respect one would give Europeans. Some Europeans felt their languages were superior, or better, and wanted Native Americans to learn to speak the European languages. But Father Rale fell in love with the beautiful Abenaki language. He wrote a dictionary of their words so their language could be shared with the world. Father Rale translated many

Martyrdom of Fr. Sebastien Rale, by Mother Mary Nealis

prayers and hymns and taught the young Abenaki people out of a catechism he wrote for them in their native tongue. Instead of expecting others to change to make things easier for him, Father Rale made the effort to learn their language.

Some Europeans forced Native Americans to be their servants, but Father Rale never allowed that. All the work he needed done in his home, he did himself. He took no food from the tribe. Instead, he drank a corn soup he made himself.

While he lived very simply and asked little for himself, he gave everything for the construction of a church for the Abenakis. It was said to be as beautiful as the best cathedrals in Europe. And why not? To Father Rale, and to our Heavenly Father, there was no difference between a European and a Native American. The church reflected this.

Soon the whole tribe was Catholic. Abenakis came from miles around to go to Mass twice a day and sing in the church choir. Father Rale—whom the Abenakis nicknamed "Black Robe"—was loved by everyone. Well, almost everyone.

Do you remember that Europeans were still fighting over territory? The French and the English were arguing over Maine, and the Abenakis—as usual—were stuck in the middle. The English were eager to grab all of Maine, but Father Rale encouraged the

Bishop Donald Pelotte, the first Native American (Abenaki) to be made, or elevated to, bishop. Bishop Pelotte was born in Maine.

Abenakis not to let the English take over their home. This angered the English government who didn't care what the "savages" wanted. To make matters worse, Father Rale had helped convert all of the Abenakis to Catholicism. The Puritan English did not like that.

Twice the English army raided Norridgewock in order to kill Father Rale, but each time he escaped into the woods with the help of his Abenaki friends. He could have fled to the safety of New France (Canada), but he always returned to his flock. He declared that only death could separate him from them.

Many times the English government tried to convince the Abenakis to betray their friend. The English offered them peace if they would leave their Faith and become Puritans. The tribe always refused.

Eventually the English got tired of talking. They attacked Norridgewock again, and this time Father Rale didn't escape. He was shot and killed. Then his beautiful "European" church was burned to the ground.

This story has a sad ending, but it's important to tell these stories. "Greater love no man has than this," says Jesus, "that he lay down his life for his friends." Since the beginning of time, the desire to own more land, property, and money than others has hurt many people. How different history would be if men and women remembered that everything we have really belongs to God, and no one person is better than another. All people are created in the image of God. Father Rale knew that. Let's pray for a world where everyone else knows this, too.

Student Workbook: Complete pg. 14.

Mysteries of History *Look! It's a Clue!*

Who were the Pilgrims and Puritans, anyway? Were they the same group of people or not?

Long ago, King Henry the Eighth of England decided to leave the Roman Catholic Church and start his own Church of England. He probably didn't guess what a religious mess he would create! But if Henry could make up his own church, why couldn't everyone else make up their own church, too? (Of course, you've probably already figured out that it's a terrible idea to leave the one and only Church that Jesus established.)

"The Landing of the Pilgrims" by Henry A. Bacon

The Puritans didn't think Henry got his church idea quite right. They were sure they could do better, so they tried to change the new church even more. The English government wasn't very happy with the Puritans, so some of them decided to leave England and live in Holland to practice their own new religion. This group of Puritans were known as Pilgrims, because they were "pilgrims" in a new land. When the move to Holland didn't work out, they decided to try somewhere else.

With some others from England, the Pilgrims boarded the ship *Mayflower* for America. Now these hard-working people finally had the freedom to worship according to their beliefs. Ten years later, more Puritans came to join them. Unfortunately, when others with different beliefs began to arrive, the Puritans-Pilgrims didn't let *them* worship freely, too!

Now that you have these clues, what more can you discover about the Puritans and Pilgrims? Put on your detective cap, and off you go!

Boston

Massachusetts

In 1620, a small group of **Pilgrims** landed not far from a spot they named **Plymouth**. It was here that they founded the second permanent English settlement in the New World (What was the first?*) and they would soon be followed by many others. **Puritans** started the **Massachusetts Bay Colony** nearby, and by 1691 the two colonies combined. Massachusetts was born! Today it is the most populous state in the New England region.

Those first Pilgrims had a hard time in this new land. Most of them weren't farmers, and the land and plants were very different from what they were used to in England. But kind Native Americans like **Massasoit, Samoset**, and **Squanto** taught the Pilgrims how to grow corn and squash and beans and pumpkins, and how to hunt the animals in the forests. Without the help of these Native Americans, the new settlers surely would have starved to death. After the Pilgrims' first harvest in 1621, they held a feast of thanksgiving to God. Because of their great friendship, the Wampanoag tribe also joined them at the feast. We continue this celebration of God's blessings every year at Thanksgiving.

This is a true and beautiful story but sadly, in the years that followed that first Thanksgiving, bloody acts of violence made lasting enemies of the settlers and Native Americans. Even people who did not fight were hurt. When you think of these fights, pray that from now on all people will do as Jesus commands us: "Love your neighbor as yourself."

*Answer: Jamestown, Virginia

"The First Thanksgiving" by Jennie Brownscombe

However, the Massachusett tribe was not killed by guns, but by something just as deadly—disease. Native Americans were not used to European diseases, so many of them died of small pox and similar diseases. By the time the Puritans arrived, only 500 Massachusett were left. Today they are all gone.

The name Massachusett means "the people beside the great hills." On the eastern side of the state is a series of 22 rises called the Blue Hills. As you move west, you'll find rich farmland in the middle of the state on the banks of the Connecticut River. (Do you remember reading about it before?) After you've crossed the river, prepare to climb the Berkshire Mountains into New York.

If you look to the southeast of Massachusetts, you'll see that the land curls into a hook shape. This is Cape Cod, full of summertime fun. In historic towns like Provincetown you can go whale watching! The hunting of whales used to be a big business here, but it is now illegal. The author Herman Melville was inspired by the time he spent here to write his great novel *Moby-Dick*. (Who is Moby-Dick?*)

*Answer: A whale

Do you see the large islands off the coast of Cape Cod? Take a spin on the nation's oldest carousel on Martha's Vineyard and

then visit Nantucket. Nantucket means "faraway land"—a trip here helps vacationers forget for a while about their busy lives back home.

Boston Tea Party

But perhaps the most important thing about this state is that there may never have been an American Revolution without Massachusetts. A center of learning, the capital city of Boston was the location of the **Boston Massacre**, when British troops fired into a crowd of Americans, killing five. A few years later, colonists were angry at having to pay taxes to the British every time they wanted a cup of tea. So patriots hatched a plan to get back at the British. They dressed up in disguises so the British wouldn't know who they were and later punish them. Then, led by Samuel Adams, they climbed aboard British ships sitting in Boston Harbor, filled with tea for the colonists. In what became known as the **Boston Tea Party**, the men dumped

all the tea in the harbor and ran off. The British wouldn't collect any taxes on that tea!

The very first shots of the Revolutionary War were fired at Lexington and Concord and many early battles in the war were fought in the state. Great men of Revolutionary times like **Paul Revere** (who galloped his horse through towns one night, warning people that the British troops were coming soon to attack) came from Massachusetts. The official state heroine of Massachusetts is Deborah Sampson, who disguised herself as a man and fought as a soldier for her country's freedom.

About this same time, a little girl was taken into slavery in Africa and sold to a family in Massachusetts. Her name was **Phillis Wheatley**. The family who owned Phillis educated her (it was unusual at this time for girls of any race to be educated), and later set her free. She became a great poet!

Fish are a natural resource that are very important for the economy of "The Bay State." Agriculture does not play a large role in the economy, but Massachusetts is the second-largest grower of cranberries in the country. What would Thanksgiving be like without cranberries?

The **American Industrial Revolution** began in Massachusetts, and it's still a major manufacturing state. Steam-powered textile (cloth-making) factories of past centuries have been replaced by modern buildings that make electrical equipment and computers. Publishing,

"The Spirit of '76" by Archibald MacNeal Willard

or the printing of magazines and books, is still a big business. And why not? America's first printing press was used here, and some of America's greatest authors like Emily Dickinson and Henry David Thoreau were from Massachusetts.

John F. Kennedy, our nation's only Catholic president, was also an author who won the Pulitzer Prize (one of literature's highest honors) for his book *Profiles in Courage*. Have you ever read a book by Massachusetts native Theodore Geisel? You probably know him better as Dr. Seuss.

Apart from books, a very unique paper product is made in the state: Crane and Company in Dalton makes all the paper used for dollar bills!

I'll bet that you have heard about our Founding Fathers, but what about Founding Mothers? Who was Abigail Adams, anyway?

The first of the Adamses in Revolutionary War history was Samuel. He was born in Massachusetts and signed the Declaration of Independence, so you know he played an important part in the Revolution. But he wasn't the only history-making Adams! Samuel had a cousin named John, a lawyer who argued and fought against unfair British rules. Needless to say, the British didn't like him much. They wanted to capture him. With his life in danger, John had to leave his farm and family during most of the war. Far from his family, he still fought to help America win its independence.

Now, John had married a fine woman named Abigail. Abigail believed that women should get a good education, and had more or less homeschooled herself. While her husband was gone during the war, she wrote a number of letters to him about the scary battles that took place close to their farm. She kept an eye on the British troops that came through the neighborhood and often passed important information about the British to John in her letters.

This made Abigail a bit of a "spy," so the British probably didn't like her much either. If she'd been caught, she would have been arrested and then who knows what might have happened. But her letters and the information she passed on helped the colonists win the war.

Because John and Abigail's activities helped America win its freedom, we think of them as two of the many "Founding Fathers and Mothers" of our great nation. And John later

"Abigail Adams" by Gilbert Stuart

became the second president of the United States! But the "Founding Mother" story doesn't stop there.

John and Abigail had a son, named John Quincy. Like the rest of their children, he was mostly homeschooled. In time, John Quincy became a lawyer, and also the sixth president of the United States. So Abigail Adams was a Founding Mother in more ways than one!

With these clues, what more can you discover about Abigail, John, and John Quincy Adams? (A search for "letters of Abigail Adams" is a good place to start your detective work.)

Student Workbook: Complete pgs. 15-16.

"While the people are virtuous [godly] they cannot be subdued; but once they lose their virtue, they will be ready to surrender their liberties to the first external or internal invader..."

—*Samuel Adams, Patriot of the American Revolution*

Did You Know? The Industrial Revolution

Long ago, there were no machines or factories. If someone wanted to buy a set of silverware, he went to a **silversmith**, a person who made things from silver. The silversmith made each fork and spoon by hand right in his own home or shop. If someone wanted to buy a woolen shirt, he went to a shirt-maker, who made the shirt by hand, right in his own home or shop. The shirt-maker bought the woolen cloth to make the shirt from a weaver, or a person who spun sheep's wool into yarn and then wove it on a loom to make cloth. With this process, it took many, many hours to make one shirt.

In the late 1700s, all this began to change. Machines that made cloth were invented. Now woolen cloth could be made very quickly in large factories with many large weaving machines. English factories that made cloth wanted more and more cotton to make more and more cloth. Cotton was grown in the American South and shipped to England.

As machinery was invented to make items from metal, other types of factories and industry joined in the "Industrial Revolution." Fewer people made things at home; more people found jobs in factories. These factories built and made products more quickly and cheaply than they could be made at home. Now people could afford to buy things that they could not buy before. The Industrial Revolution changed the way people lived and worked.

Scene in a textile mill in the northeastern U.S., 1881. A textile mill is a factory that produces cloth.

Massachusetts' Catholic Heritage

Catholicism in Boston

"Bishop John Carroll" by Gilbert Stuart

As with so many of the Northeastern states, Massachusetts' history began in England.

In the mid-1600s, Puritans in England passed strict laws that took away the rights of Catholics in Ireland. Thousands were killed, including priests and religious sisters. Many Irish Catholics were then shipped to Massachusetts as slaves. The persecution of Catholics continued in this new land. The Puritans had come to Massachusetts for religious freedom—but only for themselves.

Over a century later, the leaders of the American Revolution knew that to become a great nation all Americans must learn to respect one another. Although he was a Protestant, when General Washington passed through Boston during the war he demanded the people stop celebrating a holiday making fun of the pope.

Massachusetts Protestants worked alongside French and Canadian Catholics who came to support them in their efforts for freedom from Great Britain. After the war, some of the French sailors stayed in Boston and began to worship freely. When **Bishop John Carroll** (America's first bishop, who had been placed in charge of the whole new nation) came to visit, Governor John Hancock, a Protestant, attended Mass to show his guest respect.

There were fewer than 200 Catholics in the city at that time, but President John Adams, himself a Protestant, donated $11,000 for a new church to replace the run-down brick building the Catholics had been using. He convinced many other wealthy Protestant families to do the same. Another Protestant, Charles Bulfinch, the famed architect who designed the U.S. Capitol building, designed the new church. He refused to take money for his work. What great deeds can be accomplished when all of God's people work together!

Bishop Carroll saw that the growing Catholic population in Boston needed a bishop of its own. Pope Pius VII agreed, and made Frenchman John Louis de Cheverus the first bishop of the new See. He was succeeded by Bishop Benedict Joseph Fenwick from Baltimore. (You'll read about Benedict's brother Edward in the Ohio section.) Upon Fenwick's death, John Bernard Fitzpatrick, a native of Boston, would lead the Catholics of his home city through the worst crisis since the days of the Puritans.

It was now the middle of the 19th century, and a new political party was gaining great power. They claimed to be protecting American values, but they would have put

George Washington, John Hancock, John Adams, and Charles Bulfinch to shame. This political party was called the **Know-Nothings**. They had a funny name, but there was nothing funny about them. They hated immigrants and Catholics, whom they blamed for the problems in America. They set fire to churches and schools. In 1834, the Know-Nothings burned down a convent in Charleston, Massachusetts. Like many people who commit sin, they tried to cover their crimes by lying. When asked if they knew anything about violence towards Catholics, members replied, "I know nothing."

The people of Massachusetts knew that Catholics and Protestants could live peacefully together, but the Know-Nothings tried to make them forget that. In 1854, a Know-Nothing was elected governor of Massachusetts, and 75 members of Congress even belonged to the hateful group. Churches were burned throughout the state. Priests were run out of town by angry mobs—and tarred and feathered—that is, covered with tar and feathers!—if they returned.

This was the situation Bishop Fitzpatrick faced. His people wondered how they

should respond to this violence. Should they use violence too?

No! Jesus teaches us, "He who lives by the sword dies by the sword." Bishop Fitzpatrick urged Catholics never to use violence. When a young boy was beaten for refusing to recite a Protestant version of the Ten Commandments, the Bishop helped his family use the law to get justice peacefully.

In spite of their efforts, the Know-Nothings failed to destroy the Faith in Boston. In fact, through the grace of God, it grew stronger. Boston's Catholic community grew so large under Fitzpatrick's leadership that shortly after his death, Boston was made an **archdiocese**. The archdiocese is still growing today.

In 1689, a newspaper proudly claimed there was not one Catholic in all of New England. Today, Catholicism is the largest religion in Massachusetts and in all of New England.

Hatred and violence never win. The Puritans and the Know-Nothings have disappeared. Now Catholics and non-Catholics live side-by-side in peace.

Student Workbook: Complete pg. 17.

Did You Know? What Is an Archdiocese?

The entire country of the United States of America is divided into states, counties, and cities. The president leads the whole country; the states are led by governors; counties are led by county officials; and cities are led by mayors. The Church, too, has an order of leaders. Our Holy Father, the pope, is the "visible head," leading the whole Church. But the pope also chooses cardinals, archbishops, and bishops to lead "regions" of the Church. An archbishop leads a large region called an "archdiocese," a little like the governor leads a state. A bishop leads a smaller region called a "diocese," a little like a mayor leads a city. (The region "governed" by a bishop or an archbishop is also called a "See.") Can you name the archbishop of your archdiocese, and your diocesan bishop?

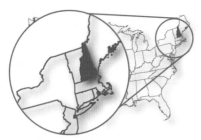

New Hampshire

Concord

Mount Washington in autumn

English settlers first came to New Hampshire in 1623. The colony declared its freedom from England ahead of the game, six months before the signing of the ***Declaration of Independence***. When it was time to sign the Constitution, nine out of the thirteen states had to agree. New Hampshire was number nine and thus the United States was born!

The Connecticut River forms the western border of this Granite State. The state's 30,000 tons of stone in the White Mountains are in demand for use in the construction of strong buildings. But in wintertime, skiers can't resist the slopes. Hold on to your hat, because

Mount Washington is one of the windiest places in the world!

Most of the people live in the southern part of the state where they work in high-technology industries like electronics and the computer industry, but more than 80% of the state is forestland, so wood products are a big business, too.

Famous New Hampshirites include Sarah Josepha Hale, who wrote "Mary Had a Little Lamb" and convinced President Abraham Lincoln to make Thanksgiving a national holiday. The poet Robert Frost was inspired by the natural wonders of his home state, and Alan B. Shepard was the first American in space and later played golf on the moon!

The unbelievable beauty of the autumn leaves attracts many visitors to this state.

American astronaut Alan B. Shepard on the moon

Rhode Island

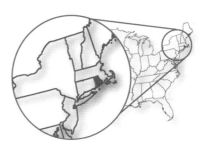

When **Roger Williams** was kicked out of the Massachusetts colony in 1636 for speaking out for religious freedom, he decided to start his own colony. Rhode Island was born!

With a history of protecting the rights of each person, this state's **delegates**—those who represent the state in Congress—refused to sign the Constitution until a **Bill of Rights** was added. When they got what they wanted, they became the last of the thirteen original colonies to join the Union. This state is officially called "The State of Rhode Island and Providence Plantations," which means the nation's smallest state actually has the longest name!

Despite its size (only 1,212 square miles), Rhode Island is one of the most densely populated states. With Narragansett Bay on the eastern part of the state, and its beautiful beaches and islands on the Atlantic, fishing is both a business and a pleasure.

The city of Newport is known for its music festivals and its more than 300 colonial homes. Here, more than a century ago, America's richest families built their "cottages" (they are really giant mansions).

Roger Williams sheltered by the Narragansett Native Americans

America's first textile mills began in Rhode Island. Clothing manufacturing is still a big business, but a lot of the factories now make electronics and jewelry instead. In the 1950s, one of these manufacturers stopped making clothes and took a chance making a new toy called Mr. Potato Head. Renamed Hasbro, the company now makes many of the world's most popular toys.

Mr. Potato Head

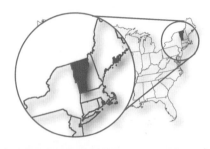

Vermont

Montpelier

"Ethan Allen and the Green Mountain Boys" by N.C. Wyeth

in 1791. This made Vermont the first state to join the Union after the thirteen original colonies.

"Vert mont" is French for the Green Mountains that run straight down the state. The Connecticut River is the state's eastern border, and a large freshwater lake in the northwest was named by Champlain after himself. There are legends that he saw a giant sea monster there, jokingly called "Champ" by the locals—but it's only a story. (Or is it?)

On the river is Burlington, the biggest city in Vermont, where computer parts and machine tools are made. However, most Vermonters live in the country. No other state produces more maple syrup.

The land we now call Vermont was discovered by French explorer **Samuel de Champlain** in 1609, but France lost Vermont to the British in the French and Indian War. Vermont's **Ethan Allen** and his **Green Mountain Boys** fought against the British in the American Revolution, but Vermont chose at first not to join the new American nation. The "Republic of Vermont" was its own country for 14 years before becoming the 14th state

In the harsh winter months, Vermonters make "sugar-on-snow" by pouring hot maple syrup on snow and then eating it with sour pickles. Does that sound like it would taste good? The only way to find out is to try it!

Sap bucket on sugar maple tree

40

Imagine you were sleeping inside a protected fort, and suddenly woke up to find that some scruffy-looking men had captured your fort. Who were these men, and where did they come from? Let's find out!

Ethan Allen, a Vermonter, had gathered his own little army of patriot farmers. They called themselves "The Green Mountain Boys." As the Revolutionary War began, it became clear that the patriots would need weapons large and small. Not far from Vermont was the British Fort Ticonderoga. There would be weapons there, and British to capture!

Ethan Allen gathered these simple farmers, the Green Mountain Boys, and off they went. Soon they were joined by more patriots, led by Colonel Benedict Arnold. This odd "army" struck while the soldiers inside the fort were still asleep. Caught by surprise, the British gave up and surrendered with barely a shot fired. Not one person was killed in the attack, and the capture of the British fort was a victory for the patriots!

With these clues, what more can you discover about Ethan Allen and the Green Mountain Boys? Grab your detective cap, and off you go!

Did You Know? The Bill of Rights

After the law of our land, the Constitution, was written, it was decided that the rights of citizens needed more protection than the Constitution offered. People still remembered that the British had arrested people for saying and writing what they wished, and took over the homes of the colonists. So the founding fathers gathered once more and came up with a list of ten rights that all citizens should have. These rights included the freedom to speak and write opinions without fear of punishment. The Bill of Rights also promised that people could freely live their Faith, without the government telling them how to practice their religion. People could gather in public without fear of arrest, and no longer could be forced to take troops into their homes if they didn't want them there! In all, there are ten rights that the Bill of Rights promises to each citizen, including you.

Student Workbook: Complete pgs. 18-24.

"Scene at the Signing of the U.S. Constitution" by Howard Chandler Christy

MID-ATLANTIC
REGION

New York

The Mid-Atlantic states are: **New York, Pennsylvania,** and **New Jersey**.

Originally explored and settled by the Dutch and the English in the 16th and 17th centuries, most of these early European settlements welcomed people of any religion. Eventually, Great Britain took complete control of the region, but the promise of religious freedom in these states still attracted different types of people from all over the world. The Mid-Atlantic states continued that tradition when they became the center of American immigration in the 19th century and beyond.

Wedged between the North and the South, the Mid-Atlantic colonies helped join the different parts of the new country during the American Revolution. Today, over 80% of this region's people live in or around cities, with America's largest city, New York City, still seen as the cultural center of the United States.

Pennsylvania

Summers are very hot and humid along the Atlantic coast. As you move farther west and away from the ocean it's still hot, but there's less humidity. On the other hand, Mid-Atlantic winters bring strong winds and lots of snow, especially near the Great Lakes. Spring and autumn are generally mild, but it is not unheard of to see people scraping an early September frost off of their windshields, or to hear the cheers of children when a freak April blizzard cancels school. One thing you can count on in the Mid-Atlantic is rain. About 35 inches of precipitation fall evenly throughout the year.

New Jersey

Turn to LESSONS ALIVE! on pgs. 25-26 of your workbook for enrichment activities.

New York

Albany ⊙

New Amsterdam, the main town in New Netherland, in 1664

While working for the Dutch, English sailor **Henry Hudson** explored a beautiful river now named for him. The Dutch were excited about the possibilities of starting a colony on the fertile soil of the bottomland that spread out all along the river. They called their colony **New Netherland**, and ruled for almost 50 years. Then, in 1664, four heavily-armed British ships arrived. Without firing a shot, the British took over New Netherland and gave it an even newer name—New York.

Native Americans lived here for thousands of years before any Europeans arrived. The Iroquois (or the Haudenosaunees) are a group of tribes who joined together into one in the 16th century; they still live in New York and Canada.

New York is graced by the Allegheny Mountains in the west and the Appalachian and Adirondack Mountains in the northeast. There are more than 200 lakes in the Adirondacks, and New York's Adirondack Park is the biggest park in the country.

Travel along the Canadian border from the southwest corner to the northeast corner of New York, and you're going to get wet! Start at Lake Erie, and then move onto Lake Ontario before diving into the Saint Lawrence River. On the eastern border moving south, you'll find Lake Champlain and the Hudson River. All throughout New York you will discover another 8,000 lakes and rivers. Can you find the Finger Lakes on a map of the state? Why do you think they have that funny name? New York is also home to the world's most famous waterfall—Niagara Falls.

Niagara Falls

All this water is not only beautiful, but very valuable. Roads were not very good in the early 1800s, and the automobile would not be invented for a long time. Wagons existed, but the roads were so poor when the land was first settled that most goods were moved by boat. However, it was a big problem figuring out how to get goods to places far from water routes.

One way to solve this problem was to build a *canal* (a man-made waterway that is something like a huge ditch or a small river). Centuries ago, with no large machinery to help in the construction, these canals were dug by strong men using muscle and shovels. Completed in 1825, the *Erie Canal* added to and joined the natural rivers and lakes in New York. The canals connected New York with the Midwest for easy trade and travel. Canals were used like "roads of water," with canal boats carrying travelers from one place to another where there were no other roads. Using the canals, farmers could send their crops to markets in cities, and cities could send supplies to stores in tiny, far-off towns. Today, the St. Lawrence Seaway makes it possible to travel nonstop by boat from the Great Lakes to the Atlantic Ocean.

In 1626, the Dutch governor bought a nearby island from the Manhattan tribe—for only $24! This was the beginning of New York City—America's largest city. Our nation's first capital (What is our capital now?*), New York is now the fourth most populous city in the world. The *Statue of Liberty* was the first sight 22 million immigrants saw when entering the United States through *Ellis Island*. With all these immigrants, New York City is called a "melting pot" of different cultures and ideas: over 800 different languages are spoken there. It makes sense that the United Nations is headquartered in New York!

Answer: Washington, D.C.

"The Erie Canal at Little Falls" by William Miller

Bronx Zoo

In New York City, you can see a play on Broadway or munch on a Coney Island hotdog and stargaze at the Hayden Planetarium. The American Museum of Natural History and the Metropolitan Museum of Art are among the best museums in the world, and there are over 4,000 animals at the Bronx Zoo!

Do you like parades? Come watch the Macy's Thanksgiving Parade and stay for New Year's Eve at Times Square, or relax in Central Park and then take in a view of the whole city from the top of the Empire State Building. The list of sights to see is endless!

Wall Street is the home of the **New York Stock Exchange**, where a lot of the world's business takes place. On September 11, 2001, terrorists flew two airplanes into the twin towers of the World Trade Center, destroying the buildings and killing 3,000 people. The world mourned with the people of New York on that sad day.

The rest of the state is very different from New York City. A quarter of the land is farms. Upstate New Yorkers grow fruit like apples, cherries, plums, pears, peaches, and grapes. More cabbage is grown in New York than in any other state, and only Vermont produces more maple syrup. Clam, lobster, squid, and flounder are fished along the Atlantic coast of Long Island. (Find Long Island on your map. Do you think the name fits?)

New York is a leader in almost every industry—especially printing, electrical equipment, machinery, chemicals, railroad equipment, buses, photographic equipment, and microchips.

2001 terrorist attack on the World Trade Center

46

Who is that lady with the weird crown, holding a torch over her head, standing on that tiny island?

That would be the noble lady called the "Statue of Liberty," on Liberty Island. This statue is a symbol of freedom; her torch light represents the light of America's liberty. Just below the statue is carved a poem that welcomes immigrants coming to America. The end of the poem, written by Emma Lazarus, reads:

> *"Give me your tired, your poor,*
> *Your huddled masses yearning to*
> *breathe free,*
> *The wretched refuse of your teeming*
> *shore.*
> *Send these, the homeless, tempest-*
> *tost to me,*
> *I lift my lamp beside the golden door!"*

Statue of Liberty

What these welcoming words must have meant to those who would begin new lives here in America! Nearby was Ellis Island, the very first place that many immigrants touched American soil.

Of course, immigrants also landed in other states and cities. They came from Poland and Ireland; from Russia and Norway; from Italy and Hungary; from China and Cuba; from Vietnam and Ethiopia; from Mexico and the Holy Land; from every country in the world.

Most of these people were very poor, but they brought great riches to their new land. How is this possible? The riches they brought were new ideas and cultures, often a great faith, and a willingness to work hard to make better lives for themselves as Americans. These new ideas, cultures, faith, and hard work made the immigrants richer, and enriched our entire nation as well. The United States of America is truly a nation built by immigrants!

With these clues, what more can you discover about Ellis Island, Emma Lazarus, and the Statue of Liberty? Do these clues help solve some of the mystery of your family's arrival in the United States, too? How did our country's history of immigration change the way your family lives today? How might your life have been different if your ancestors had never come to this land?

Student Workbook: Complete pg. 27.

New York's
Catholic Heritage

Who was the first American saint? That's not an easy question to answer, but to try we must look to New York.

The French priest **Father Isaac Jogues** spent five years ministering to a group of Hurons in what is now upstate New York. In 1642, Father Jogues' companions were captured by an unfriendly tribe. Father Jogues could have escaped, but he gave himself up so his friends— who would face great suffering—would have a priest with them. Women of this unfriendly tribe chewed off both of Father Jogues' index fingers before he and his friends were forced into slavery. Later, when René Goupil, one of the lay missionaries, made the sign of the cross over a sick child, an angry tribesman killed him.

With the help of some Dutch sailors, Father Jogues escaped back to France, but he immediately wished to return to care for the people who had treated him so badly. He knew they needed the love of Christ most of all.

When he returned to the village where he had once been a slave, he helped make peace between the warring French and the tribe. But not everyone was happy to see him return. Father Jogues was captured and beheaded. The next day, when Jean de Lalande, a lay missionary, tried to find Father Jogues' body he was also killed.

The **North American Martyrs**—a group which includes Father Jogues and his companions—were declared saints in 1930. Many people consider Saints René Goupil, Isaac Jogues and Jean de Lalande to be the first American saints because they were **martyred**—killed because of their faithful witness to Jesus—in New York.

North American Martyrs, by Mother Mary Nealis

St. Frances Xavier Cabrini

St. Kateri Tekakwitha

St. Elizabeth Ann Seton

In spite of Father Jogues' tragic death, many Native Americans embraced Jesus and His Church. The pure Faith of **Kateri Tekakwitha** has earned her the nickname "The Lily of the Mohawks." **Canonized**—declared a saint—in 2012, Saint Kateri is considered by many to be the first American saint—she is the first Native American saint, and the first saint born in what would one day be the United States.

By 1889, the holy work of the Missionaries of the Sacred Heart and its founder **Frances Xavier Cabrini**—who was twice turned away from joining religious orders due to poor health—soon attracted the attention of many people in her native Italy and eventually the Pope himself. She had dreamed as a little girl of becoming a missionary to China, but Pope Leo XIII had different plans. "Look not to the East, but to the West," he declared, and soon Mother Cabrini found herself on a ship headed towards New York harbor. On the ship she began ministering to the poor Italian immigrants coming to America for a new life, and she never stopped. Canonized in 1946, she is considered by many to be the first American saint because she was the first U.S. citizen declared a saint.

When she was born in 1774, in New York City, no one would have imagined Elizabeth Ann Bayley would become a saint. Born into a wealthy Protestant family, she married William Magee Seton, from an equally wealthy family. They didn't marry for money, but for love. They had five children before tragedy struck—William died of a terrible disease called tuberculosis while the couple was visiting Italy.

Elizabeth stayed in Italy for six more months with friends of the family—the only Catholic family she had ever met. She had been raised to believe Catholics were bad people, but the Filicchis showed her the truth through their gentle example. When she returned to New York she converted to the Catholic faith. Her friends and family turned her away forever, and now she had to struggle to survive.

She tried to open a school in New York City, but the prejudice, or hatred against Catholics, that she faced made this dream impossible. A visit from Bishop John Carroll from Baltimore helped strengthen her faith and a priest friend suggested she start a school in the Maryland city. In 1809 Elizabeth established the Sisters of Charity, dedicated to opening schools and orphanages all along the East Coast. Many people consider **Elizabeth Ann Seton** the first American saint because in 1975 she became the first native-born American citizen to be canonized.

So who is the first American saint? Does it matter?

The real question is: what is an American? As a nation of **diversity**, a place of many people from different backgrounds and cultures, there is no one right answer. It is only fitting that America's saints should remind us of that great fact.

A Nation Built by Immigrants

Haym Salomon, Jewish Revolutionary War Patriot

After immigrating from Poland to New York, Haym Salomon became a successful businessman. Not long after the Revolutionary War began, Haym began spying for the American side, quietly giving information to the Continental Army. He was captured by the British, put in prison, and later sentenced to hang. But Haym escaped!

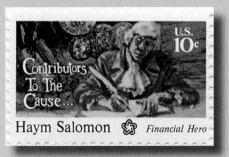

As the war continued, General George Washington had no more money to pay his troops. He could not even buy food for them! Haym Salomon came to the rescue. He not only set up business deals to make money to buy supplies for Washington's Continental Army, but also gave much of his own fortune to help win the war. Haym Salomon was a true patriot who treasured freedom more than riches.

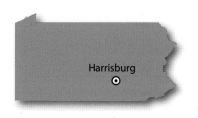

Harrisburg

Pennsylvania

Back in 1682, King Charles II of England owed William Penn's family some money. The king couldn't pay, so he gave Penn some land in North America instead. Penn was embarrassed when the new colony was given the name of Pennsylvania—he was afraid people would think he was prideful—but the name stuck.

William Penn was a humble man who believed people should be able to choose their religion without being forced. He was a Quaker, but people of any religion were allowed to settle in his colony. Today, Pennsylvania still has people of many religions living together—including a large population of Amish.

We know who "Penn" is, but what about "Sylvania?" This Latin word means "forest land." It fits Pennsylvania perfectly! Over 9% of the woods in the whole country are in Pennsylvania. Most of Pennsylvania is in the hilly Appalachian Mountains, but as you move west you are greeted by the **plains**, or flat lands, and valleys of the Allegheny Plateau.

If you ever construct a building, don't forget the keystone, the stone that "locks" together all the stones that support the building. Without the keystone, your building might fall apart! Pennsylvania is known as "The Keystone State." In the time of the Thirteen Colonies, six colonies were above Pennsylvania and six colonies were below it. During the American Revolution, it was obvious that, if Pennsylvania didn't join this new country, the country would be divided into two separate parts! So Pennsylvania became the "keystone" that kept our new country together.

Today, Pennsylvania borders six states, a Great Lake (Which one?*), and shares a water border with Canada. On the southern border is the **Mason-Dixon Line**—a sort of imaginary boundary separating the North from the South. Can you see why Pennsylvania is still "The Keystone State?"

"Treaty of William Penn with Indians" by Benjamin West

*Answer: Lake Erie

Most of the planning for the American Revolution and the development of our new nation happened in Philadelphia. A major port on the Delaware River on the southeast border of the state, Philadelphia is Pennsylvania's largest city and now the fourth largest in the United States. From 1790 to 1800, it was our nation's second capital city. (Do you remember our first?*) Independence National Historic Park preserves **Independence Hall** where the Declaration of Independence and the Constitution were both signed. After you visit there, go see the Liberty Bell—the most famous symbol of American independence. (If you get hungry be sure to try a Philadelphia Cheese Steak!)

In 1861, ongoing arguments between northern and southern states exploded into a violent **Civil War**, a war which was not fought because a foreign country was attacking, but because two parts of our one nation—the North and the South—were at war with each other. For four years, Americans fought against Americans; sometimes even families were split in two, with some members fighting for the South, and others fighting for the North. Even the family of President **Abraham Lincoln**, the president of the United States, was divided! Four brothers of Mary Todd Lincoln, First Lady of our country, fought in the South's Confederate Army. Two of her brothers were killed in battle.

*Answer: New York City

Above: Liberty Bell

Left: "The Declaration Committee" (Benjamin Franklin, John Adams, and Thomas Jefferson) meeting at Jefferson's lodgings in Philadelphia to review a draft of the Declaration of Independence, by Jean Ferris

Many fierce battles were fought in Pennsylvania, including the **Battle of Gettysburg**. More soldiers died in that battle than in any other Civil War battle. It was here that President Abraham Lincoln later delivered his **Gettysburg Address**—perhaps the greatest speech in American history. It has inspired millions. Read it and you'll be inspired too.

"Four score and seven years ago our fathers brought forth on this continent a new nation, conceived in liberty, and dedicated to the proposition that all men are created equal.

Now we are engaged in a great civil war, testing whether that nation, or any nation, so conceived and so dedicated, can long endure. We are met on a great battle-field of that war...."

—*from Abraham Lincoln's* Gettysburg Address

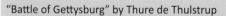
"Battle of Gettysburg" by Thure de Thulstrup

Pennsylvania farmers raise cows, chickens, and pigs. They grow corn, oats, soybeans, and more mushrooms than any other state. Sometimes called "The Workshop of the World," Pennsylvania is a major manufacturing state. Miners dig for minerals including limestone and iron **ores** (rocks that are used to make metal) which go into manufacturing Portland cement and pig iron. As the fourth largest coal mining state in the country, Pennsylvania helps fuel our nation's factories and homes.

Edwin Drake was the first to successfully drill oil in Titusville. However, Pennsylvania is best known for its steel industry. Pittsburgh has been the leader in steel production since the 1800s. Pennsylvanians also work to make medicine, cars, electronics, machinery, books, and forest products.

Are you a chocolate lover? Lampposts shaped like Hershey Kisses line Chocolate Avenue in the city of Hershey, home of the American chocolate industry. After you've stuffed yourself there don't forget that Pennsylvania produces more pretzels and potato chips than any other state. If you can't move after all that snacking, why not sit still and do some coloring with Crayola crayons? They come from Pennsylvania too. (Just don't eat them!)

Pennsylvania's **Benjamin Franklin** was one of the world's greatest thinkers— perhaps you've heard of his experiments with electricity? He was also a Revolutionary War patriot, an author, a musician, an inventor, a statesman, a postman, a fireman... It would take up this whole book to list his many accomplishments!

However, Pennsylvania's oddest citizen is Punxsutawney Phil. On February 2nd each year people wait to see if this groundhog will see his shadow. If he does, legend says winter snow will continue for six more weeks. What do you think about that?

Did You Know? The Mason-Dixon Line

Not long before the Revolutionary War, Charles Mason and Jeremiah Dixon surveyed, or carefully measured, the lands where Pennsylvania and Maryland meet. The line, or border, that divided these two states was called the Mason-Dixon Line. This was not a line that can be seen, like a line drawn on paper. Instead, it is the boundary between two states, just as your state and county have borders, too. But the Mason-Dixon Line became very important as a division between slave and free states. It was also a line that divided the North (the Union) and the South (the Confederacy) in the Civil War, that sad and terrible war that very nearly tore our nation in two.

Pennsylvania's
Catholic Heritage

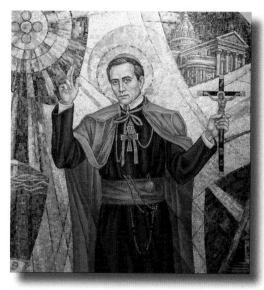

Mosaic of St. John Neumann

Inspired by the missionary adventures of Saint Paul, **John Neumann** longed to spread the Gospel in faraway lands. In 1836, the young man from Prague, Bohemia (now the Czech Republic) got his wish and travelled to the United States. As a newly ordained priest, he spent several years ministering to the needs of German and Native American Catholics in New York. In Baltimore, Maryland—a place where slavery was still legal—he helped support a group of black nuns who wanted to teach African-American children.

His years of good service attracted the attention of Pope Pius IX, who named him Bishop of Philadelphia—a huge diocese with thousands of German, Irish, and Italian Catholics, yet with very little money. Despite their poverty, his new flock planned a fancy parade to welcome him. The Bishop asked that the parade be canceled and the money used to build a school instead. He believed the little money the diocese had should always go to the people, never to him. For the rest of his life, he wore the same worn-out boots that he had since his days in Bohemia. He refused to use diocesan money to replace them.

From his first day as Bishop, Neumann demonstrated his belief that his job was to serve the people of his diocese personally. During his first year as Bishop, he visited more than half of Philadelphia's parishes to celebrate Mass, hear confessions, and just talk to people. He already spoke German, but he insisted on learning Italian and Irish too so he could speak to all in their native languages. He believed people of all ethnic groups should be treated with equal respect.

Neumann was the first bishop in the United States to create a Catholic school system. The Know-Nothings (remember them?) burned down many of these schools and convents, but in the end Bishop Neumann built over 200 schools and many convents with nuns to teach in them. He built so many churches that a new one was finished almost every month!

When the Bishop died in 1860, a little girl in his diocese named **Katharine Drexel** was only two years old. From a family of millionaires, Katharine and her sisters were guaranteed a life of ease. However, her parents were faithful Catholics who knew God had blessed them with riches only to help others.

When her parents died, Katharine and her sisters were guaranteed millions of dollars every year for the rest of their lives. What

St. Katharine Drexel, courtesy of the Sisters of the Blessed Sacrament

would you do with that much money? Katharine could have spent it all on herself, but her parents had taught her well. She immediately began donating thousands of dollars to the Bureau of Catholic Indian Missions.

Just as John Neumann had worked with Native Americans in his early days, Katharine felt that Native Americans—who were often hated, discriminated against, and even killed—deserved love and respect.

Also, like Bishop Neumann, she saw how poorly African-Americans were often treated. The horror of slavery was a recent memory and African-Americans still faced prejudice and violence. Like the good Bishop before her, she knew all these things were wrong.

In 1891, Katharine founded a new religious order called the Sisters of the Blessed Sacrament for Indians and Colored People. (Today "colored people" seems an offensive term, but it was considered respectful in Katharine's

time.) Over 100 like-minded sisters soon joined her mission to pray for and bring the powerful help of the Eucharist to Native Americans and African-Americans. Within her lifetime, the sisters opened 12 schools for Native Americans and 50 for African-Americans.

You might think this was easy for Katharine because she was a millionaire, but she wasn't a millionaire any more. She gave away all her money; she and her order lived in complete poverty. But they didn't need money to be happy. They had God's love.

Katharine retired in 1937 due to a serious illness and spent the last 18 years of her life in quiet prayer. No doubt, Bishop Neumann watched over her then as he did her whole life. Now they both watch over Pennsylvania—and the world—together. John Neumann was declared a saint in 1977, and Katharine Drexel in 2000.

New Jersey

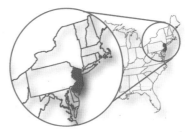

New Jersey was originally settled by the Dutch, but by 1664 the English had taken this land for themselves. The name of this state goes back to the English Civil War (1642-1651), when England's royal family was in danger: two men hurried the royal family to safety, hiding them on England's Isle of Jersey. To thank the men, James II, Duke of York, gave them this far-away land taken from the Dutch. The new owners thought *New Jersey* would be a fitting name for their colony.

New Jersey's huge neighbors, New York and Pennsylvania, make New Jersey look small, but this state played a big part in the American Revolution. More than fifty battles were fought here, and George Washington's famous crossing of the Delaware River is one of the defining moments of American history. New Jersey proudly became the third state in 1787.

Inviting beaches and seaside resorts line this state's Atlantic shore. The properties in the game *Monopoly* are named for real places in Atlantic City, where you can chew on saltwater taffy as you stroll along the city's famous boardwalk. Perhaps you'd like to visit

"Washington Crossing the Delaware" by Emanuel Leutze

Thomas Edison, inventor

the Pine Barrens, but don't be fooled by the name—over a thousand animals and plants live in these forests and swamps.

The "Garden State" grows blueberries, cranberries, peaches, lettuce, bell peppers, potatoes and tomatoes on its nearly 10,000 farms! Others have jobs in industry and produce medicines, chemicals, and oil products. Insurance is another big business.

Thomas Edison—a homeschooled inventor who made the first practical electric light bulb, a type of movie camera, and many other items that improved life for people around the world—dreamed up most of his inventions at Menlo Park; Campbell's began ladling out their famous soups here in 1869. Catholic ***Antonin Scalia***, United States Supreme Court Justice and descendent of Italian immigrants, was also born in New Jersey.

Antonin Scalia, Supreme Court Justice

I'll bet you thought that the Revolutionary War was fought against the British. So why did General George Washington attack the Germans in New Jersey? Let's find out!

Not only British and Americans fought in the Revolutionary War! French General Marquis de LaFayette and Polish General Kazimierz Pulaski fought for American freedom alongside our troops. Baron von Steuben, from Prussia, trained General Washington's troops at Valley Forge, Pennsylvania.

The British had others helping their side, too. German troops, called Hessians, were hired by the British to fight against the Americans.

One famous battle between American troops and the Hessians occurred near Trenton, New Jersey, in the very early morning hours of December 26, 1776. The German troops had just the day before celebrated Christmas by staying up late and partying (big mistake—they should have gone to Holy Mass instead).

During the night, while the Hessians slept, General Washington and his troops crept closer. Early the next morning, as the Germans snored, Washington attacked. The Hessians flew out of bed in shock and soon surrendered, some probably still in their jammies. After the war, many of the

"The Nation Makers" by Howard Pyle

German soldiers decided that they liked the freedoms offered by America, and chose to stay here.

Now that you have these clues, what more can you discover about people who came from other countries to fight in the Revolutionary War?

Student Workbook: Complete pgs. 28-30.

Canada

Lake Winnipeg

Manitoba

Lake Nipigon

Ontario

NORTH DAKOTA

Missouri R.

Lake Sakakawea

★ Bismarck

Lake Superior

MINNESOTA

WISCONSIN

Lake Michigan

SOUTH DAKOTA

Lake Oahe

★ Pierre

Lake Huron

Saint Paul ★

MICHIGAN

★ Lansing

Missouri R.

IOWA

Madison ★

Lake Erie

NEBRASKA

Platte R.

Des Moines ★

Missouri R.

OHIO

Lincoln ★

INDIANA

Springfield ★

Indianapolis ★

Columbus ★

Topeka ★

ILLINOIS

Ohio R.

WEST VIRGINIA

KANSAS

Jefferson City ★

Missouri R.

MISSOURI

Ohio R.

KENTUCKY

Arkansas R.

OKLAHOMA

ARKANSAS

TENNESSEE

Missouri R.

MISSISSIPPI

GEORGIA

TEXAS

LOUISIANA

ALABAMA

FLORIDA

"Marquette and Joliet Exploring the Upper Mississippi" by Frank Zeitler

Indiana · Michigan · Ohio · Illinois · Wisconsin · Missouri

The Midwestern Region

Nebraska · Iowa · Kansas · Minnesota · North Dakota · South Dakota

The Midwestern Region

Midwesterners have often been thought of as representing the "average" American but, really, the Midwest is home to people from many different backgrounds and occupations. In this region, you'll find motorcycle-riding cowboys, Amish buggies, spaceships, ancient Native American earthworks, and unbelievably tall, steel-framed buildings towering far above cities.

Early settlers of the Midwest arrived from New England, the Mid-Atlantic States, and the South. In the 19th and 20th centuries, steel mills and other factories attracted immigrants, as well as African-Americans from the South seeking a new life. With these settlers and immigrants, Midwestern cities grew quickly. Today, some of these cities are the biggest and most bustling in the country, yet they sit comfortably alongside miles of peaceful, unspoiled farmland.

The Mississippi River roughly divides the Midwest into two smaller regions—The East North-Central region and the West North-Central region.

East North-Central
REGION

On the eastern side of the Mississippi you'll find the East North-Central Region, where **Indiana, Michigan, Ohio, Illinois,** and **Wisconsin** are located.

The first Europeans to explore this area were the French, who lost their land claims to the British after the French and Indian War in 1763. (You remember reading about the French and Indian War when we studied Maine.)

After the American Revolution, the new United States took possession of this mostly unsettled land. Known as the Northwest Territory, the East North-Central states were all carved from this vast wilderness.

The East North-Central states are known as the "Great Lakes States" because each state is connected to one of these five lakes—the largest freshwater lakes in the world. In 1825, the Erie Canal created a waterway connecting the Great Lakes to the rest of the country in the east, making it easy to ship goods and products. Soon huge manufacturing cities sprang up around these waterways. Many factories have closed in recent years, but cities in the East North-Central region are still some of the nation's most important centers of manufacturing.

The East North-Central region is blessed with some of the richest soil in the world and plenty of relatively flat land, so farmers also flocked to this region throughout the 19th century. Today, corn and other crops grown here still help to feed the world.

This region has four distinct seasons. Summers can be very hot. In the winter, children sled and make snowmen while their parents shovel and plow a lot of snow!

Turn to **LESSONS ALIVE!** on pgs. 31-32 of your workbook for enrichment activities.

Indiana

Michigan

Ohio

Illinois

Wisconsin

Indiana

Indianapolis

Long ago, Native American tribes like the Miami, Potawatomi, Kickapoo, Mascouten, Delaware, and Shawnee filled Indiana—the land of the Indians. As American settlers began to move west, trouble erupted here. Years of violent battles between these tribes and the U.S. military came to an end in 1811. After General William Henry Harrison defeated the Shawnee at the famous **Battle of Tippecanoe**, white settlers began flooding in. Indiana gained statehood in 1816, but most of the Native Americans were forced to leave their lands. By 1850, the land of the Indians was no more—but the name remains to remind us of the first people to live in this ancient land.

Indiana is filled with beautiful lakes and streams, with two important rivers. The Wabash River flows southwest across the middle of the state, turns south to form part of the western border with Illinois, and then flows into the Ohio River. The Ohio River then creates Indiana's southern border. (With your finger, can you trace the river's path on the map?) The Wabash is the longest river east of the Mississippi and its beauty inspired Indiana's state song, "On the Banks of the Wabash, Far Away."

Indiana's relatively flat geography and rich soil help farmers grow many different crops. Corn is number one— Indiana is especially known for its delicious popping corn. Soybeans, wheat,

"The Lookout" by Albert Bierstadt

tomatoes, grapes, melons, and mint are also major crops. Dairy cows, pigs, and poultry are raised in Indiana, too. Over 95% of these agricultural goods leave Indiana to be sold in different places all over the country.

Mostly, Indiana is a manufacturing state. Northwest Indiana produces more steel than anywhere else in the country, while Indiana oil refineries change crude oil into gasoline and other useful products. Automobile manufacturing and the production of chemicals, rubber products, and electrical equipment are other major industries, and Indiana is the number two state for the number of people who work in pharmaceuticals (making medicine). Mining is also an important industry—more coal and limestone are mined in Indiana than in any other state.

While huge factories in cities like Gary, Fort Wayne, and South Bend bring in money for Indiana's economy, they used to create a lot of pollution. Some of that pollution went into Lake Michigan. Today, however, the people in the factories work hard to keep their state clean for people and animals. For example, the clean waters of Lake Michigan draw beachgoers to the popular vacation spot of Indiana Dunes National Lakeshore.

Indiana is also a sports-fan's dream state. The first high school basketball

Indianapolis 500 Mile Race

teams were formed here. Indianapolis—the capital of Indiana—is home to the world-famous Indianapolis 500 auto race. More people attend this high-speed race than any other sporting event in the country.

The Notre Dame "Fighting Irish" is a football legend. Indiana's most famous college was founded by a group of Holy Cross priests. (Notre Dame means "Our Lady" in French. Can you guess who "Our Lady" is?) The rules of the university state that a priest must always be the president of this Catholic university.

People from Ohio are called Ohioans. Citizens of Virginia are Virginians, and Texans live in Texas. What do you think we call a person from Indiana? An Indianan? An Indianian? It's neither of these. The official name for a person from Indiana is a Hoosier. There are lots of stories of where the funny name came from, but no one really knows for sure. What do you think?

Student Workbook: Complete pg. 33.

Indiana's
Catholic Heritage

St. Theodore Guerin

Have you read about Jesus' miracles? As Catholics, we believe in these miracles by faith, even though we didn't see them with our own eyes. Jesus says, "Blessed are they that have not seen, and yet have believed."

Sadly, not everyone has this faith. One day, someone may say to you, "God is not real. The Bible is just a fairy tale. If it were true, why don't miracles happen today?" What will you say? Do miracles still happen today? Read on to find out.

At the very end of the French Revolution, in a little town called Etables, France, Anne-Therese Guerin was born. Instead of playing with other children, she preferred to walk along the shoreline by herself praying and thinking about God. Even as a child she longed one day to serve Jesus as one of His nuns.

In 1823, she joined the Sisters of Providence and took the name Sister Theodore. Maybe because she spent so much time caring for sick people, she caught a terrible disease called smallpox. Medicine cured her, but it had some bad side effects, leaving her painfully weak and tired all the time. Think how surprised she was when she was asked to found a motherhouse and novitiate for new sisters across the ocean in the wilderness of Indiana!

After a dangerous journey, Sister Theodore and five other nuns finally arrived in Indiana on October 22, 1840. In these woods so far from France, Sister Theodore was now Mother Theodore—the leader of a new community of women she called the Sisters of Providence of Saint Mary-of-the-Woods.

The sisters' first year in Indiana was particularly difficult. Many of the pioneers did not like Catholics—especially nuns. The harsh winter winds often threatened to knock over the small wooden farmhouse where the postulants, or new sisters, lived. Food was hard to come by and life-threatening illnesses were common. Then, when it seemed things couldn't get worse, a huge fire broke out. The little food the sisters had was burned away. Now they had nothing. Through all this hardship Mother Theodore comforted her new family. She often reminded them, "With Jesus, what shall we have to fear?"

Despite these early disasters, Mother Theodore and the other sisters opened their first school that summer. Many people in Mother Theodore's time thought women didn't need an education, but Mother Theodore knew better. She built a college just for women. Today it is called Saint Mary-of-the-Woods College—the oldest Catholic college for women and one of the oldest women's colleges in the whole nation.

Over the next few years, the sisters opened more schools throughout Indiana and Illinois. They formed two orphanages and opened a place where the very poor could get free medicine.

Mother Theodore would live for sixteen years after her arrival in Indiana, but even after her death, the other sisters knew she still watched over the Sisters of Providence from Heaven.

In 1908, nearly sixty years after Mother Theodore's death, Sister of Providence Mary Theodosia Mug, who had been stricken with a deadly disease, prayed at Mother Theodore's tomb to be healed.

When Sister Mary awoke the next day her illness had vanished.

About a hundred years later a man named Phil McCord had an important job as a facilities manager for the Sisters of Providence. Unfortunately, his vision was growing weaker and weaker, making his job and his life more difficult each day.

McCord passed by the Church of the Immaculate Conception in Saint Mary-of-the-Woods all the time because of his job, but in January 2001 something different happened. He heard organ music and suddenly found himself entering the Church. He had a strong feeling that he should pray to Mother Theodore to help him through an operation he was going to have on his eyes. McCord admits to feeling a change right away and by the next morning his eyesight had completely recovered. He now has perfect vision!

Do miracles still happen today? The answer is yes!

Sometimes people think the lives of these holy men and women are just made-up stories, but they are not. Have faith! These great men and women of the past are still with us right now, watching over us in Heaven and doing God's will. When we pray, miracles can happen—even today.

Mother Theodore was officially declared a saint in October 2006.

Michigan

Lansing

The first European explorers of Michigan were Catholics from French Canada, who were later followed by a great priest, *Father Jacques Marquette*. In 1668, Father Marquette founded the first European settlement in Michigan. (Don't forget his name, because you'll read more about him soon!)

Easy water access led to a profitable *fur trade* between the French and Native American tribes like the Ojibwa, the Ottawa, and the Potawatomi. (Only a few centuries ago, animal furs were in great demand. These furs were used to make warm clothing and hats at a time when people had very poorly heated homes and no heated cars in which to travel long, frozen miles. People who had to travel great distances on foot or by horse-drawn wagon, and were caught in sudden snow storms, sometimes froze to death! You can imagine why most people wanted to own a warm, protective coat. Many of the furs for these coats were supplied by rugged mountain men and Native Americans who spent months alone in a dangerous wilderness, trapping animals for their valuable and often life-saving furs.)

The French lost Michigan to the British after the French and Indian War in 1763. Unhappy with British control, Chief Pontiac of the Ottawa fought a bloody war against the European

Fur trapper, by Frederic Remington

68

empire. To avoid further violence, the British government passed the **Royal Proclamation of 1763**, creating a boundary between British colonists and Native American tribes. This treaty was unpopular among British colonists. (Anger over the treaty may have been one of the causes of the American Revolution.) The Royal Proclamation ended when the new United States won the land after the Revolution. The Michigan Territory was formed in 1805, and settlers from New England poured in. In 1837, Michigan became the 26th state.

The name Michigan comes from the Algonquian word "michi-gama," which means "Large Lake." If you look at a map of Michigan you can see why the name was given. Michigan touches four of the five Great Lakes, and the whole state is split into two parts thanks to Lake Michigan. This makes Michigan the only state divided into two peninsulas. (A **peninsula** is a piece of land surrounded by water on three sides, but still connected to the mainland.)

As if the Great Lakes weren't enough, Michigan is sprinkled with over 11,000 other lakes and peppered with thousands of islands. To top it all off, Michigan is home to 150 splashing waterfalls. So if you like swimming and boating and fishing, Michigan is the state for you!

The Great Lakes provide Michigan with a range of different climates that allow

for growing many different plants. Only California grows a more diverse variety of crops. Corn, soybeans, and wheat are grown in Michigan, and many dairy products are produced. No other state grows more cherries or blueberries.

As you move farther south, Michigan transforms into an important industrial region. Most people who live in Michigan live in this lower part of the state, which is called the Lower Peninsula. Detroit, which is famous for automobile manufacturing, is located here. Men like Henry Ford and Ransom E. Olds started their car factories close by, earning Detroit the nickname "Motor City" or "Motown." Soulful music of the Supremes, the Temptations, and other 1960s pop groups is sometimes called Motown too, because of the Detroit record company that helped make the sound popular around the world.

Henry Ford in his first automobile, the "Quadricycle"

Skiing on sand

Besides automobiles, Michigan also produces metal products and non-electrical machinery. The city of Grand Rapids, home of the Kellogg's and Post companies, manufactures more breakfast cereal than anywhere else in the world. Do you have any cereal in your house? Go look at the package's back. Chances are your cereal was packaged in Grand Rapids, Michigan!

Some people who think of Michigan think only of the large, industrial cities like Detroit, but over half of Michigan is covered by lush and beautiful forests.

Large herds of deer, elk, and moose wander through this peaceful scenery. Although the northern part of Michigan (called the Upper Peninsula) has sawmills and a big fishing industry, it is mostly visited by campers and people on vacation. In the summer you can camp, swim, boat, or fish. Would you like to come back in the winter and try snowboarding, tobogganing, and ice fishing? Bring a warm coat!

One of the most popular places to visit is Mackinac Island—a tiny island in between the two parts of Michigan. You can only get there by boat and, once there, no cars are allowed. (Can you imagine what would happen if they had a rule like that in Detroit?)

Have you ever heard of anyone skiing on sand? On the shoreline of Lake Michigan in the Lower Peninsula is a giant hill of sand called Sleeping Bear Sand Dune that is so big some people actually ski down it!

Fr. Gabriel Richard

Fr. Gabriel was born and ordained in France, but sent to serve the Church first in Illinois and then in Michigan. He built schools and taught our Holy Faith both to the French who had settled in the area and to the Mohawks as well. When the British captured Fr. Gabriel during the War of 1812, Shawnee Chief Tecumseh came to his aid. Later, while caring for victims of cholera, an often-deadly disease, Father Gabriel himself caught the disease and died. He had truly poured out his life in service to God's children.

Michigan's
Catholic Heritage

The Story of
Fr. Jacques Marquette

Jacques Marquette was one of the greatest explorers in the history of the world—and one of our greatest priests!

In 1666, the French priest's dream of preaching to Native Americans in far off North America came true. He spent the cold winter of 1668 in a Native American village the French called Sault Ste. Marie. The small mission he founded here became the oldest European settlement in Michigan and the entire Midwest.

From Sault Ste. Marie he traveled—mostly on foot—preaching Christianity and living for many years with the Huron and Ottawa tribes along the coast of Lake Superior.

One day, a group of friendly Illini tribesmen arrived in a boat, telling tales of a great river that seemed to flow on forever. Marquette wondered if this "great river" might flow all the way to the Pacific Ocean. More importantly,

he wondered about the many people along the river who may never have heard the word of God.

While planning to seek this great river, Marquette and his friends were attacked by an unfriendly tribe. They fled to a new home on the island of Mackinac. The mission Marquette founded here didn't look very fancy, but that didn't matter. Of all his missions, Mackinac became the one Marquette thought of as "home."

Marquette loved Mackinac, but he never forgot about the great river. Imagine his excitement when explorer **Louis Joliet** arrived and asked Marquette to join him in finding it! In May 1673, Marquette, Joliet, and five others began their adventure in a couple of birch-bark canoes.

The first people the explorers met were Marquette's old friends the Illini. The tribe presented them with a peace pipe to use on their journey. This was an important symbol and a touching gift. Many Europeans had been cruel to Native Americans, but their native friends knew that Marquette and Joliet were peaceful men.

By the middle of June, Marquette and Joliet caught their first sight of the "Great River." The Algonquian word for "Great River" is "Misi-ziibi." Can you guess what we call this river today? The Mississippi!

The party quickly figured out that the Mississippi does not go all the way to the Pacific Ocean. Since the river bent south they thought it might flow into the Gulf of Mexico instead. This time they were right. They continued to follow the river and on their way discovered the Missouri River (the longest river in the U.S.) and the Jefferson River.

The explorers had almost reached the Gulf of Mexico when they received warning from the Illini that **hostile** (extremely unfriendly and dangerous) Native Americans and their Spanish friends were waiting up ahead to attack. Remember: Joliet and Marquette did not want to fight people. It was time to return home.

On their return trip, they visited a large Illini village where Marquette was asked to stay and teach. Unable to stay behind and leave his team, Marquette moved on but he knew God wanted him to return to that village.

Eventually, Marquette said goodbye to Joliet to return to the Illini village. On the way he became very sick, but he was determined to go on. At last, he reached the tribe around Easter 1675. When the Illini finally received the blessed Eucharist, Father Marquette knew he had completed his mission. His life was coming to an end. His last wish was to return to the place he thought of as home—his simple mission at Mackinac.

Fr. Marquette on his trip down the Mississippi River

Fr. Marquette and the Indians, by Wilhelm Lamprecht

Two Illini offered to help Marquette on his long journey home. They were still far from Mackinac when Marquette spotted a small stream. How tiny it must have seemed when compared to the roaring Mississippi, but Marquette saw God's beauty in all His creation—big and small. Now so weak he could no longer walk, he asked his friends to carry him to the shore of that humble stream. Far from home, he laid down his head and died.

Two years later a party of Illini arrived at Mackinac. They carried with them the bones of their friend and priest, Father Marquette. They had brought him home, at last.

Why did they do this? Jesus says, "Love one another as I have loved you." As you already know, Europeans often fought with Native Americans. But Father Marquette was not like this. He was only one man, but one person—with the love of Christ—can change the world forever.

Student Workbook: Complete pgs. 34-35.

Ohio

Columbus

"Ohio" is an Iroquois word which means "something beautiful" or "beautiful river." Early European explorers agreed with the Iroquois, some saying that Ohio was so beautiful it seemed like the Garden of Eden. But what a shock when deep in the Ohio woods they then discovered a huge hill in the shape of a giant snake! (It's not really a hill, but the

Snake Mound

world's largest effigy mound—a sculpture of an animal made out of raised earth.) This giant "snake" was built by an ancient tribe over a thousand years ago. If you're ever in Peebles, Ohio, go see it and try to solve the mystery of why it was built. Nobody knows for sure.

Although the French and British had argued for years over control of Ohio, the United States would found Marietta,

the first non-native settlement, in 1788. Marietta was the first of the river towns to spring up along the Ohio River—the Iroquois' "beautiful river" that now forms Ohio's southern border. Ports on this river helped Ohio's economy grow.

After being defeated at the Battle of Fallen Timbers in 1794, Native Americans were forced to allow more American settlement. In 1796, settlers from New England founded Cleveland on the shores of Lake Erie—Ohio's northern border. (Today, music lovers visit to see the Rock and Roll Hall of Fame or to hear the world-famous Cleveland Orchestra.) In 1803, Ohio became the 17th state.

The completion of the Erie Canal in 1825 helped make Ohio a huge center of trade in the 19th century. In fact, canals threaded across farmland, carrying farm products to small towns and cities. However, the invention of railroads (which didn't depend on sources of water for travel) led to the abandonment of the canal system. Yet even today, Lake Erie connects to the

St. Lawrence Seaway

"The Underground Railroad" by Charles Webber

Atlantic Ocean by the man-made St. Lawrence Seaway, and Ohio ships still carry coal and iron ore over Ohio's waterways and out to the world.

The Ohio River was once the border between states that allowed slavery (slave states) and those that did not (free states). Before the Civil War, slaves who escaped on the **Underground Railroad** compared the Ohio River to the Jordan River. (Can you figure out why?*)

The Underground Railroad was a network of people who helped runaway slaves escape the South to freedom in the North. The Underground Railroad Freedom Center in Cincinnati (Ohio's biggest riverfront city) honors this piece of Ohio history.

Ohio is one of the country's most important industrial states. Iron, steel, oil, machinery, chemicals, and office equipment are all produced here. Only Michigan makes more cars. Ohio is also the largest producer of appliances, electrical equipment, and plastics in the United States. Rubber companies Goodrich, Goodyear, Firestone, and General Tire were all founded in Akron—the "Rubber City." Even today, no other state produces more of this valuable product.

With these many businesses, you might get the feeling that Ohio is one big city, but that's not the case. Ohio does have large cities, but in between them are little towns and vast farmlands. Ohio farms produce abundant corn, soybeans, and other crops, making

Orville and Wilbur Wright

agriculture one of the biggest parts of the state's economy. In southeastern Ohio, coal miners help fuel the world.

Throughout the countryside you will find the world's largest Amish community—people who reject most modern technology and live much like people did more than one hundred years ago, before electricity, cars, radios, television, or computers. Wendy's hamburgers and Smucker's jelly make for yummy Ohio treats! After your snack, stop by the Pro Football Hall of Fame in Canton, a paradise for pigskin fans.

Many famous people have hailed from Ohio. Eight presidents were born or lived in the state, tying with Virginia for the record and the title "Mother of Presidents."

Orville and *Wilbur Wright*, the inventors of the airplane, were from Dayton. You can visit one of their old bicycle shops if you're in town, and then stop by the National Museum of the United States Air Force to see the world's largest collection of military aircraft.

As if the invention of the airplane wasn't enough, a record-breaking twenty-four astronauts got their start in Ohio. Ohioan John Glenn was the first American to orbit the Earth, and Neil Armstrong was the first man to walk on the moon.

Finally, if you're reading this book by the glow of an electric light bulb, you can thank Ohioan Thomas Edison, a genius who created thousands of new inventions, many of which we still use every day!

Neil Armstrong, astronaut

76

Orville and Wilbur Wright's family name was very fitting for their work. Since "Wright" seems to have nothing to do with the bicycles and airplanes made by the famous Wright Brothers, what can this possibly mean? Let's find out!

"Wright" is actually a very old word used to describe someone who created something with his hands. A wheelwright made wheels; a shipwright made ships.

Long ago, most people didn't have family names. A thousand years ago, in the Middle Ages, Wilbur and Orville would simply have been known by their first names. But sometimes this could get confusing. If someone asked about "John," and there were fourteen Johns living in town, how would people know which John they were asking about?

So people would say, "John the wheelwright" if John made wheels; or "John by the church," or "John from the church" if this particular John lived by or worked for the church. After a time, the names were simply shortened to "John Wheelwright" or "John Church."

If John were a farmer, guess what family name became his? "John Farmer"! Or if he had once been a slave, but was now free, he might become "John Freeman."

At other times, people were named by their skin color—"John Brown"—or by another physical characteristic—"John Short."

Now that you have these clues to a "mystery of history," perhaps you can do a bit of detective work to figure out where your family name came from!

Student Workbook: Complete pg. 36.

"I know this world is ruled by infinite intelligence. Everything that surrounds us—everything that exists—proves that there are infinite laws behind it. There can be no denying this fact. It is mathematical in its precision."

—Thomas Edison

Ohio's
Catholic Heritage

The Story of Bishop Flaget

Do you remember the Parable of the Lost Sheep? Maybe **Bishop Benedict Joseph Flaget** was thinking of this story while he searched through the hostile wilderness of what we now call Ohio.

In the early 1800s, Bishop Flaget was put in charge of the largest diocese in American history—an area the size of 10 modern states, including the future state of Ohio. Today, Ohio is home to millions of people, but in Bishop Flaget's time there were very few settlers and even fewer Catholics.

With his many responsibilities, Bishop Flaget might have found it easier to ignore the handful of Catholics in far-away Ohio—but God doesn't always want us to do things the easy way, but the *best* way: His way.

Bishop Flaget knew God doesn't want even one of His children to be separated from His Church, so he saddled his horse and ventured deep into the wilderness. He searched long and hard, but he couldn't find any Catholics. Again, it

would have been easier to give up and go home. However, like the Good Shepherd of the Parable, he kept on searching.

One day he was overjoyed to discover a small group of Catholic families in a place now called Somerset. These families begged him to send them a priest. Without delay, Bishop Flaget sent for a wonderful Dominican priest called Edward Fenwick.

The families at Somerset had no church, so when Father Fenwick arrived he had to say Mass in someone's house. Nobody minded. Everyone was just happy finally to receive the Eucharist. Then Father Fenwick had to leave, but he promised to return and help the families build a real church. Two years later, he made good on his promise.

Meanwhile, Bishop Flaget had reached Cincinnati—at this time not a city, but little more than a few log cabins. Inside one of these cabins, Bishop Flaget held the first Mass for the small Catholic community.

Your local church probably offers daily Mass, but do you remember how long the families at Somerset had to wait in between visits of Father Fenwick? Two years! Try to imagine how sad it must have been to wait years and years for the Eucharist. Bishop Flaget knew that a permanent church must be built as soon as possible, but here he faced a greater challenge than when he first trekked into the Ohio wilderness.

Some non-Catholics in Cincinnati didn't like Catholics. They had made it against the law for a Catholic church to be built in the city! On top of that, the small group of Catholics didn't have enough money to build a church anyway. For a third time, Bishop Flaget could have done the easy thing and given up. There were not a lot of Catholics in Cincinnati, so who would care if they were forgotten? I think you know the answer to that one: God would care!

Bishop Flaget helped the Catholics in Cincinnati get assistance from other Catholics in the east. With this help, the Catholics were able to pay for a small plot of land just outside the city limits. A kind Catholic in Kentucky donated wood for construction. These huge logs had to be strapped to rafts in order to cross the Ohio River and then were carted for miles and miles by ox-drawn wagons. It was a dangerous journey, but the wood made it safely.

It took a lot of hard work, but eventually the church was finished. The plain building looked more like a barn than a church, but the Catholics in Cincinnati saw it as the most beautiful building in the world. Why do you think they felt that way?

While the church was being built, Bishop Flaget enthusiastically recommended that Ohio be made its own diocese. Can you guess who he recommended as the first Bishop of Cincinnati? Good old Father Fenwick!

As you've read, there were only a few Catholic families in Ohio, but over time more and more Catholics arrived. Today, Ohio has one of the largest Catholic populations in the United States. It all started because Bishop Flaget listened to God, and—like the Good Shepherd— never gave up searching for even one lost sheep.

Father Edward Fenwick blessing the first Catholics in Ohio

What does Chicago have to do with a legend about a cow kicking over a lantern in a barn? Let's find out!

The summer of 1871 was fierce, hot, and dry across most of the Midwest. Since houses, stores, sidewalks, and even some roadways were made of wood, there was plenty of very dry wood to fuel a fire if one should start.

Legend has it that a cow kicked over a kerosene lantern in the barn of one Mrs. O'Leary, starting a fire that nearly destroyed the city of Chicago. Pushed by strong winds, the flames burned a path almost four miles long right through the city. Men, women, and children ran for their lives. For safety, many went to stand in Chicago's rivers and nearby Lake Michigan.

Still, the terrible fire killed about 300 people and destroyed about 17,000 buildings. The fire was finally stopped a few days later when a light rain fell. (A newspaper reporter later admitted that he had made up the story about the cow!)

As horrible as was the Great Chicago Fire, there is more to this mystery. You see, shortly before the Great Chicago Fire began, the town of Peshtigo, Wisconsin, and several neighboring towns, also burned down. About 2,000 people died in these fires, many more than lost their lives in the Chicago fire. But by the time newspapers learned of these disasters, the Great Chicago Fire had already captured their attention. The news reported only on the "big city" fire. What lesson do you suppose we can learn from this?

Now that you have these clues, grab your detective cap and see what you can discover about the Great Chicago Fire and the Peshtigo Fire, too!

Chicago in flames

Illinois

Illinois is nicknamed "The Prairie State" because of its flat and fertile farmland, where hard-working farmers plant and harvest corn, soybeans, wheat, oats, barley and sorghum. Mining is important in the southern part of the state, but manufacturing provides more than ten times the income of any other business. Most industry is centered in Chicago, the third largest city in the United States and home to O'Hare Airport, the busiest airport in the world.

The catastrophic **Great Chicago Fire** of 1871 destroyed much of the city, but you'd never know it now. Chicago's streets are lined with over a dozen of the tallest skyscrapers in the world, including the Willis Tower (formerly called the Sears Tower), the tallest building in the country. At 110-stories high, tourists can stand on a transparent platform that juts out away from the building, making them feel like they are hanging in mid-air. Would you be brave enough to look down?

At the Field Museum meet Sue—the world's largest skeleton of a *Tyrannosaurus rex*! Chicago is also the birthplace of Mickey Mouse creator Walt Disney.

Ronald Reagan was the only president born in Illinois, but President Abraham Lincoln spent most of his life here before leading the nation through the Civil War. Illinoisans are proud to call their state "The Land of Lincoln."

Monument in Lincoln Park, Chicago, Illinois

Fr. Augustine Tolton

Fr. Augustine Tolton was born into slavery in 1854. His family left his Missouri birthplace for Illinois, where Augustine grew up. He was ordained to the priesthood in Rome, and returned to Illinois where he served God's people until his death in 1897.

Sue, the world's largest skeleton of a *Tyrannosaurus rex*

Wisconsin

Madison ⊙

Have you eaten any cheese, milk, or butter today? Chances are it came from Wisconsin. Most of America's dairy products are produced in this state, giving it the nickname "America's Dairyland."

So many dairy products come from Wisconsin that some people think everyone in Wisconsin lives on a dairy farm, but that isn't true. Most people live in cities; about one-third of the state's population lives in or around the big city of Milwaukee—one of the world's most important beer-producing cities and also the home of Harley-Davidson motorcycles.

Wisconsin has more than 15,000 lakes, and its lush forests contribute wood for Wisconsin's successful papermaking industry. Those who grow the trees used in papermaking are careful to plant more than they cut down, so future generations can enjoy Wisconsin's natural beauty.

The Ringling Brothers performed their first circus acts in Wisconsin—visit the Circus World Museum in Baraboo for a "big top" adventure. Next, zoom by the annual EAA AirVenture in Oshkosh for America's biggest air show. Harry Houdini, the world's most famous magician, grew up in Appleton.

One Sunday in 1881, when drugstore-owner Edward Berner drizzled chocolate syrup over some ice cream, the "sundae" was born! Four years later, when fifteen-year-old Charlie Nagreen smashed a meatball between two slices of bread he may have accidentally invented the hamburger!

Student Workbook: Complete pgs. 37-39.

A Nation Built by Immigrants

Polish Immigration to Wisconsin

In the mid-1800s, the country of Poland was attacked and ruled first by the Russians and then by the Prussians. These foreign governments made life very difficult for the Polish people, so thousands left all behind seeking freedom and a new life in America. A good number of these immigrants settled and farmed in the Midwest, building homes and Catholic churches in their new communities. You may even know the story of one Catholic Polish family who settled in Wisconsin. The author Anne Pellowski has written the story of her family's immigration from Poland in *First Farm in the Valley: Anna's Story*.

West North-Central
REGION

On the western side of the Mississippi River is the West North-Central Region. The states in this region are: **Missouri, Nebraska, Iowa, Kansas, Minnesota, North Dakota,** and **South Dakota**.

The West North-Central States were formed mostly from the *Louisiana Purchase*—a huge parcel of land which France had first explored and claimed, but then sold to the United States in 1803. The Louisiana Purchase more than doubled our nation's size at that time. In fact, most of the land that came with the purchase is nowhere near our present state of Louisiana!

These states all lie within the *Great Plains*—a huge stretch of flat prairie. Oddly, the region was once nicknamed "The Great American Desert," because people thought no crops could grow there. However, farmers armed with clever farming techniques and modern technology transformed the Great Plains into an agricultural powerhouse.

Today, the West North-Central States supply the entire world with 18% of its wheat. Because of the huge amount of wheat and corn produced in these states, they are often called "America's Breadbasket."

America's two most important and longest rivers meet in this region: the Missouri River flows southeast through the West North-Central states, emptying into the Mississippi River. This water access allows goods to be shipped easily around the country.

The temperature in the West North-Central region varies greatly over the year. Summers can be as hot as 100 degrees Fahrenheit, while winter temperatures in this region can dip to -60 degrees Fahrenheit (in North Dakota)! Unlike the East North-Central region, with its abundant rain and snowfall, the climate becomes increasingly dry as you move west across the Great Plains.

Turn to **LESSONS ALIVE!** on pg. 40 of your workbook for enrichment activities.

Missouri

Nebraska

Iowa

Kansas

Minnesota

North Dakota

South Dakota

Put on your detective cap—you have some thinking to do!

Imagine that you live in St. Joseph, Missouri, and your grandparents live in California. Your grandparents write you a letter, inviting you to come for a visit, but they must know your answer by April 14. You see that their letter was sent on March 12, 1860. Today is April 3, 1860. How many days did it take their letter to reach you?

If the year were 2013, how many ways would you have to contact your grandparents to let them know that you were coming?

In 1860, there was no email, no texting, no Skype. There were no telephones. The only way to send a message was by mail, and it took at least three weeks for mail to be carried by stagecoach from Missouri to California. (Look at a map to see how many states are between Missouri and California. That is how far a stagecoach would have to carry your letter.)

Would there be enough time for your message to reach your grandparents? (Did you use the clues to figure which day your letter would arrive if you sent it on April 3rd?) No, there is no way that your letter would reach your grandparents in time.

But wait! You hear that tomorrow something called "The Pony Express" will start carrying the mail. With this express, or "very fast" mail service, letters will be carried not by stagecoach, but by a brave teen-aged rider on a speedy horse. Why, letters will now travel the distance in only ten days!

This young rider gallops his horse for 10 or 15 miles to a Pony Express station out in the middle of nowhere. A rested horse awaits him. There, our brave young man leaps from his tired, sweaty horse, swiftly pulling a small bag of mail from the saddle. Throwing the mailbag onto the saddle of the fresh horse, the rider leaps on, and gallops away to the next station.

Pony Express riders sped through dangerous territory. There were no roads, but plenty of wild animals like bears, mountain lions, wolves, and rattlesnakes. Across mountains, blazing deserts, and through winter blizzards, day and night they galloped to deliver the mail. Each rider traveled about 75 miles before passing the mail on to a new

Pony Express by Shannon Stirnweis, *www.shannonstirnweis.com*

rider and fresh horse at yet another Pony Express Station.

But there is more to the story: the Pony Express went out of business after only a year!

About fifteen years before the Pony Express, **Samuel Morse** invented a machine called the **telegraph**. A telegraph could send a tapped-out code of "clicks" over wires. Different taps were used for each letter of the alphabet. Telegraph operators could spell out messages using this code and send the message to another telegraph station hundreds of miles away. These messages traveled

Samuel Morse, inventor

over the wires much more quickly than letters ever could.

By October of 1861, telegraph wires stretched across the United States; messages no longer took days to cross the country, but only a few minutes. The Pony Express was no longer needed, thanks to a man named Samuel Morse and his **Morse Code**.

With all these clues, maybe you can find out more about Morse Code. Learn the code, and send a few tapped messages to your family or friends; all you need is a pencil or stick to tap on a hard surface.

Missouri

This book calls Missouri a Midwestern state, but many people say it seems more like a Southern state. St. Louis, Missouri is sometimes called "the western-most eastern city," but Kansas City, Missouri is claimed to be "the eastern-most western city."

Confused? In a way, Missouri is a "little USA" that often represents the makeup of the whole country better than any other state. For example, the people of Missouri have predicted the winner of almost every presidential election since 1904. Does this mean Missouri has no identity of its own? Not at all! Read on to learn more about this northern, southern, eastern, western, incredibly unique state called Missouri.

Louis Joliet and Father Jacques Marquette were the first Europeans to get a glimpse of Missouri. (Do you remember reading about their adventures in the Michigan section?) Years after their explorations, the United States bought Missouri as a part of the Louisiana Purchase.

The two largest rivers in the United States meet in Missouri. The mighty Mississippi moves along the eastern border of the state, while the Missouri River creates the northwestern border. The Missouri River flows in a ragged line down to Kansas City, where it then turns east and cuts across the middle of the state. The Missouri River connects with the Mississippi River just north of St. Louis. You already know how important waterways are to business, but a few years after the Louisiana Purchase something unexpected happened that changed Missouri forever.

In 1807, a man named **Robert Fulton** made successful a powerful new form of transportation called the *steamboat*. This new boat, much larger than previous river boats, could easily carry more passengers and cargo up and down rivers at speeds never before imagined. Robert Fulton and his steamboat would change the world and make Missouri a huge center for business.

Have your parents ever given you and your brothers and sisters a choice that you had

Workers loading cotton onto a steam boat

a hard time agreeing on? Maybe they said that you could vote whether you had pizza for dinner or hamburgers, but no one could agree. Did you come to a *compromise*, or make a decision that seemed the most fair to both sides? Perhaps you decided to have pizza this week and hamburgers the next, or found another compromise.

The senators and representatives that represent us in Congress have to find compromises, too.

You remember that in the 1800s, slavery was allowed in southern states, but not in northern states. Slaves mostly worked on huge southern farms, or plantations. These plantations were the most important part of the southern economy, or the way people worked and made money to take care of their families. (Unfortunately, slaves weren't paid!) Southern plantation owners felt that, without slavery, plantations would go out of business. If plantations went out of business, most of the South would go out of business!

In Congress, senators and representatives from both southern and northern states voted on laws that affected all the states. Because the northern states were against slavery and the southern states were for it, there were often big arguments in Congress.

By the 1820s, America had grown far beyond the original thirteen states into new territory. People who settled in a new territory soon wanted it to become a state. But the people in the South didn't want more northern states where slavery was illegal, and the people in the North didn't want more southern states where slavery was legal. So Congress kept arguing! How could they come to an agreement?

So many people moved to Missouri that it soon became eligible for statehood, but in Congress arguments raged over whether it should be a free or slave state. Finally, in 1821, the **Missouri Compromise** brought Missouri into the Union as a slave state and Maine in as a free state. This kept the number of free and slave states equal, with the same number of senators in the Senate. Unfortunately, this compromise did not solve the problem of slavery, which would eventually cause a bloody civil war. Surprisingly, although it was a slave state, Missouri fought on the Union side in the Civil War.

Missouri was once the border between civilization and wilderness, the starting point for pioneers in wagon trains beginning their long journey west. The Oregon and Santa Fe Trails both began at Independence, Missouri.

In 1804, **Meriwether Lewis** and **William Clark** here began a famous journey of discovery. America had just bought a vast territory from the French, the Louisiana Purchase. No one really knew what this new territory held. Might there be a river that could be used as a waterway, so people could travel all the way across the country by boat? What kind of people lived in this new land? Were there new plants or animals there, or

Lewis and Clark with Sacagawea, by N.C. Wyeth

perhaps precious gold and silver? President Jefferson decided to send Lewis and Clark to explore all the way to the Pacific Ocean. Their trip took two years, and covered nearly 8,000 miles!

In those 8,000 miles, they mapped new rivers, mountains, and trails. They met native tribes who helped them along the way, and some that were not so friendly. The **Lewis and Clark Expedition** gathered important information about this new territory, information that made settlement much easier for **pioneers,** or the first settlers who later came to this unsettled region.

The **Pony Express** once carried mail on horseback from St. Joseph, Missouri, to distant California, while infamous outlaws like Jesse James roamed the land. Today, the 630-foot-high stainless steel Gateway Arch in St. Louis stands to symbolize Missouri's history as the "gateway to the west."

Northern Missouri is rather flat and suitable for farming, but the southern region rises up into the tree-lined Ozark Mountains. This popular vacation spot is famous for its thousands of deep, dark caves. Missouri has more caves than any other state. At last count there were over 45,000, but more are discovered each year.

With over 100,000 livestock, produce, and grain farms, Missouri has more farms and ranches than any other state except one. (Which state do you think this is?*) Missouri farmers grow soybeans, corn, rice, and cotton. Beef, pork, poultry, eggs, and dairy products are also produced.

Cars, aircraft, and even spacecraft are built in Missouri. The production of chemicals and electric equipment also provides jobs. Missouri is first in the nation in lead and zinc production, and number one in limestone—a natural resource used to make cement.

Have you ever received a greeting card in the mail? If you have, look at the back. Was it made by Hallmark, the world's largest greeting card company? Hallmark was founded by Joyce Clyde Hall in Kansas City, Missouri.

Hannibal, Missouri, was the hometown of Samuel Clemens—better known by his pen name **Mark Twain**. Perhaps the greatest American author (and certainly the funniest), his books like *The Adventures of Tom Sawyer*, *The Adventures of Huckleberry Finn,* and *Joan of Arc* are still enjoyed today.

Jesse James, outlaw

Gateway Arch

*Answer: Texas

87

Painting of St. Rose Philippine Duchesne, located at Villa Duchesne, St. Louis, Missouri

Catholic Heritage

St. Rose Philippine Duchesne

When she was a little girl growing up in far-off France, **Rose Philippine Duchesne's** family was visited by a Jesuit who told tales of French missionaries spreading the Faith in the Louisiana Territory. From that moment on, Philippine knew God was calling her to the New World. However, her own country of France needed her first.

When Philippine was a teenager, France underwent a bloody revolution. The leaders of this Revolution **banned**, or outlawed and made illegal, the Catholic faith and brutally murdered thousands of priests, monks, nuns and faithful lay people. Unable to formally enter the religious life under these conditions, Philippine placed herself under a simple form of religious rule caring for the sick and visiting priests in prison. She risked

her life every day teaching children the Faith.

After the Revolution, the laws against Catholics were repealed (reversed) and a peasant girl named **Madeleine Sophie Barat** founded a new religious order called the Society of the Sacred Heart. A meeting between Philippine and Mother Barat began a great friendship; each woman always felt the other was the better example of Christ's love.

For twelve years, Sr. Philippine helped rebuild the Faith in France, but she still longed to go to America. One day, the bishop of the Missouri Territory visited Mother Barat. As he discussed privately with her his desperate need for nuns, Philippine burst into the room, fell to her knees, and begged to be sent. With a smile, Mother Barat readily agreed.

Philippine was nearly fifty years old when she and four other sisters finally reached Louisiana on May 29, 1818— the Feast of the Sacred Heart. The five sisters took a boat up the Mississippi River to St. Louis, Missouri—at this time just the beginning of a frontier town. The sisters founded an orphanage and a novitiate encouraging native-born Americans to join the Society. In nearby St. Charles, the sisters built the first free school west of the Mississippi River.

Despite her accomplishments, Philippine felt that nothing seemed to go right. She tried and tried, but could never learn English very well. There was never enough food, water, or firewood. Worst of all, due to a lack of students, the school in St. Charles shut down.

Philippine blamed herself for all the failures of the Society. She constantly gave credit to the other nuns, but thought of herself as useless. All around her knew the truth of her sacrifices. When she did sleep, she slept in a closet. Usually she stayed up late mending the children's clothes. When she finished, she would spend the night on her knees adoring the Blessed Sacrament. Philippine fasted in the morning and only allowed herself the scraps from the children's plates in the evening. Whenever there were jobs to be done, she gave the easy tasks to others and saved the hardest for herself.

Despite constant trouble with money, several more foundations were opened under Philippine's leadership. She even managed to reopen the house at St. Charles. Hundreds of children soon filled the Society's schools.

When Philippine was 70 years old, she retired to the house in St. Louis. One day, a priest who came to speak with some young nuns about establishing a mission among the Potawatomi tribe spotted Philippine praying silently. He demanded she come too! Although surprised, Philippine agreed to go.

Just as she had struggled with English, Philippine could not learn the Potawatomi language. Again, she felt useless.

Unable to teach, she instead spent eight hours a day in prayer before the tabernacle. At first, the Potawatomi found this old lady strange and stared at her. Eventually, some were moved to kiss her tattered habit. Soon they began to bring her gifts and treat her with great honor. She became known among the people as Quah-Kah-Kanum-ad, which means "The Woman Who Prays Always."

Philippine brought the Potawatomi the Love of Christ, yet never spoke a word. This is the power of prayer. God often uses our weaknesses to accomplish great things. Philippine's last words sum up the source of her holiness: "Jesus, Mary and Joseph, I give you my heart, my soul, and my life—oh yes, my life, generously!"

Rose Philippine Duchesne was officially declared a saint in 1988.

Student Workbook: Complete pg. 41.

Nebraska

Lincoln

Most visitors to Nebraska are left in awe by its incredible flatness. Even the word "Nebraska" means "flat river" in the language of the Otoe tribe. (While it's true that most of Nebraska is flat, at its western border with Wyoming and Colorado the land rises more than a mile high, where harsh blizzards often form.)

The Otoe's "flat river" was renamed the Platte (French for flat) by early explorers. The Platte runs from east to west straight through the middle of the state, flowing out of the Missouri River. The Missouri River makes up Nebraska's eastern border and around 450 miles of its northern border, too. The Platte and Missouri Rivers have saved many farmers from the deadly droughts that sometimes strike the state.

The French were the first Europeans to explore and claim Nebraska, another state that resulted from the Louisiana Purchase. The Lewis and Clark Expedition passed through in 1804, describing vast, dry prairies. These descriptions led most people to believe that growing crops there was impossible. Little did they know!

Seeing small value in settlement, the American government reserved the land for Native Americans. However, Nebraska's flatness provided a perfect natural highway—in the 1840s, thousands of wagons passed through to follow the Oregon and Mormon Trails to points farther west. Then in 1848, the discovery of gold in California inspired more and more Americans to travel west through Nebraska. Some people never made it to California, but stayed in Nebraska.

As more settlers arrived, the American government convinced most Native Americans to give up their land, although native resistance continued in some parts of Nebraska until 1877. Today, Nebraska is still home to the Omaha and Ho-Chunk tribes, who live mostly on reservations in Thurston County, where they make up the majority of the population. While early settlers forced these tribes' ancestors onto these reservations, today tribal politicians and state officials try to work together to solve problems.

In 1854, members of Congress passed the ***Kansas-Nebraska Act***, officially creating

"Prairie Indian Encampment" by John Mix Stanley

the neighboring territories of Kansas and Nebraska. Part of this law said the two territories could vote on whether they wanted slavery or not. Many people saw this as going against the Missouri Compromise, which stated that slave and free states must be equal in number. Anger over the Kansas-Nebraska Act led to violence, and is now seen as one of the causes of the Civil War.

Remember, Nebraska was not thought to be suitable for farming, so few settlers were interested in moving here. The **Homestead Act of 1862** changed that: the American government promised 160 acres of free land to anyone who would live on it for five years. The prospect of free land was worth the challenge, and settlers stormed in. In 1867 Nebraska became the 37th state.

Due to a lack of trees, these early settlers had to build their homes out of dirt and sod bricks! (Sod bricks are simple squares cut from dirt, with grass still attached.) These settlers knew they needed trees,

so they started planting them everywhere they could. Today, Nebraska is filled with trees. In fact, Nebraska is now home to the nation's only National Forest planted entirely by people. To celebrate their success, Nebraskans in 1872 celebrated a new holiday called Arbor Day, dedicated to planting trees. Now it is not only a national holiday, but a holiday celebrated in many countries around the world. Is it any surprise that Nebraska is sometimes called "The Tree Planters' State"?

Clever farmers with new agricultural techniques proved wrong all those who thought crops wouldn't grow here. Today, Nebraska is one of the most important farming states in the country—over 95% of the state is covered with farms and ranches! Major crops are wheat, hay, sorghum and soybeans, and so much corn is grown here that the official nickname of Nebraska is "The Cornhusker State." Nebraska's flat plains are also filled with more types of grass than in any other state, which is perfect for raising cattle.

Most manufacturing in this state is related to agriculture. Breakfast cereal is a major industry, and the city of Omaha is the country's leader in meatpacking.

Have you ever tried Nebraska's official state soft drink? In 1927, Edwin Perkins of Hastings invented Kool-Aid in his mother's kitchen!

Sod house in winter

Nebraska's
Catholic Heritage

The Story of Fr. Flanagan

Father Flanagan designed his "Workingman's Hotel" in Omaha, Nebraska as temporary housing for victims of a terrible tornado and drought that had recently hit the area. When the United States entered World War I in 1917, most of the men still living in the Workingman's Hotel joined the war effort. However, homeless men from all over the country soon arrived to replace them. These men were different from the victims of the tornado and drought. Many of them had a history of violence, drunkenness, crime, or all three.

Most were afraid of these men, but not Father Flanagan. He wondered why some men were good and some men were bad. He took the time to listen and tried to understand them. He met thousands of homeless men and noticed that no matter what their story, they all had one thing in common: not one had grown up in a loving family.

Father Flanagan thought back over his life. When he was born years ago in

Ireland, he was so sick everyone thought he would die. Sitting by the fire, his grandfather held him against his chest for days until the baby's health returned. Father Flanagan's most precious childhood memories were of his father—a gentle man who prayed the Rosary with his son as they searched in the rain for lost sheep. Later, when sickness forced Father Flanagan to quit seminary, his precious sister Nellie nursed him back to health twice so he could return to his vocation.

A question arose in the young priest's mind—if he had not had such a loving family as a boy, could he have wound up living in the Workingman's Hotel rather than running it?

That summer, Father Flanagan went to the juvenile courthouse. He picked seven orphaned boys who were in trouble for breaking the law many times and started meeting with them three times a week. He taught the boys a better way to live, not through punishing them, but by showing them love. A lot of people thought he was wasting his time and felt those bad boys should be in jail. The priest explained, "I don't believe that a child can be reformed by lock and key and bars, or that fear can ever develop a child's character."

That November, Father Flanagan started taking troubled boys into his care. By Christmas, the boys—now numbering over 150—had moved into a large house. These orphaned boys spent their first true Christmas in Father Flanagan's home—a Christmas filled with love, the first real love these boys had ever known.

Soon, one house was not enough. In 1921, when Father Flanagan came into possession of a large farm, he founded a whole new town—**Boys Town**! Still, some people thought Father Flanagan was wasting his time with bad boys. He would say, "There are no bad boys. There is only bad environment, bad training, bad example, bad thinking."

Spencer Tracy won the Academy Award for Best Actor portraying Father Flanagan in the 1938 movie *Boys Town*. Tracy donated his award to Boys Town where it is still on display. After World War II, President Harry Truman asked Father Flanagan to represent the United States in an attempt to help war orphans across Europe. Despite his fame, Father Flanagan never lost sight of his humble mission. "It's God's work," he would remind everyone, "not mine."

During his lifetime, Father Flanagan helped more than 6,000 children get a better start in life. Today, Boys Town helps over 1.4 million young people and their families every year. Now there are Boys Town locations in ten states and Washington, D.C. Dozens of youth programs around the world are also based on Father Flanagan's work and ideas.

All of this great work began with a simple priest who loved God and family. He had a special love for Mary—the mother of all orphans, the unloved, and the forgotten. He prayed the Rosary every day just as his father had taught him so many years ago. He never forgot those happy childhood days—days that were recreated for millions and millions of boys and girls because of Father Flanagan's priestly love.

Fr. Flanagan celebrating Christmas with residents of Boys Town

93

Iowa

Des Moines

Covered bridge in Madison County, Iowa

Thousands of years ago, giant **glaciers**, huge frozen "mountains" of ice, lumbered across what we now call Iowa. When the glaciers melted, they left behind some of the best soil in the world for farming. Sometimes called "The Food Capital of the World," this state grows more corn than anywhere else in our country and raises more hogs than anywhere else on earth!

Have you ever enjoyed the sweetness of a shiny Red Delicious apple? You can thank Iowa's Jesse Hiatt, who first cultivated this perfectly named snack. Farming is such a huge part of Iowa's economy that even most of the state's manufacturing—such as the country's biggest popcorn factory in Sioux City—is in some way related to agriculture.

Iowa is the only state bordered completely by two major rivers. With the Mississippi River on the east, and the Missouri River on the west, Iowans can ship their goods across the country with ease.

This state is considered one of the safest in which to live, and is also a great place to have fun. Tourists like to see Iowa's famous covered bridges. More than a million people visit the Iowa State Fair each August to see livestock exhibitions and eat blue-ribbon-winning pies. Meredith Willson's musical *The Music Man* is a loving tribute to his childhood years in early 20th-century Iowa.

Kansas

"Home on the Range," the state song of Kansas, reminds us of a time when herds of wild buffalo roamed free across the Great Plains. "Old West" towns like Dodge City still stand, but today they are modern cities.

Kansas grows more wheat than any other state and has so many silos that other states send their grain to Kansas for storage. Is it a surprise that Kansas is called "The Breadbasket of America"?

Despite their success, Kansas farmers have endured many hardships. In the 1930s, Kansas suffered through a years-long, crop-killing drought called the **Dust Bowl**, when hot winds blew parched soil across the prairie, burying farms and driving farmers out of business. Many families lost their homes, farms, and income. Today, farmers must still worry about tornados—more twisters hit Kansas than any other state. In addition to farming, the economy of Kansas includes the meatpacking, car, and airplane industries.

Famed pilot Amelia Earhart was from Kansas, and President Dwight Eisenhower grew up here. One of the bravest people from Kansas was 9-year-old **Linda Brown** from Topeka. Who was Linda Brown?

Once-productive family farm, covered by dunes of sand and dust during the Dust Bowl

In some states in the 1950s, African-Americans were not allowed to go to school with white children. Students were **segregated**, or separated simply because of the color of their skins, and sent to separate, or segregated, schools. Linda was one of these students. Her parents rightly felt that she should be able to go to any school she wanted. In the court case **Brown v. the Board of Education** the **United States Supreme Court** declared that treating children differently because of the color of their skin is wrong. Because of this Supreme Court ruling, and a brave little girl named Linda Brown, children of every race can go to school together.

Fr. Benjamin Petit and Archbishop Charles Chaput

The Potawatomi were one of many Native American tribes forced by the government to leave their homes to make room for settlers. These tribes were made to travel hundreds of miles and more, often by foot, to a new and unfriendly land. Many died on these long, sad marches which became known as the "Trail of Tears" and the "Trail of Death." Yet, there were those who willingly joined the tribes on these marches. One of these was Father Benjamin Petit. He went with the Potawatomi, many of whom were Catholic, when they were moved to Kansas. Father Petit suffered along with the tribe and helped in any way that he could. He especially cared for the sick and dying.

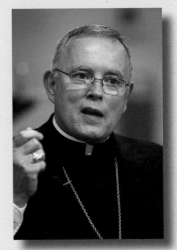

Archbishop Charles Chaput

Some of the Potawatomi who survived this sorrowful move to Kansas were the ancestors of Archbishop Charles Chaput. Archbishop Chaput was the first person of Native American heritage to be elevated to archbishop.

"The Trail of Tears" by Robert Lindneux

Minnesota

Saint Paul ⊙

St. Paul Winter Carnival

This "Land of 10,000 Lakes" has more like 15,000 bodies of water and millions of acres of lush forests. Here in Minnesota, the mighty Mississippi River begins—as a trickle of water only two feet deep! The Mississippi might not look like much here, but the river grows wider and deeper as it flows down the state, before dividing the twin cities of Minneapolis and St. Paul.

In a Minneapolis park you can see Minnehaha Falls, made famous by Henry Wadsworth Longfellow's classic poem *The Song of Hiawatha*. Each year thousands bundle up for icy fun at the St. Paul Winter Carnival. However, if you really want to shiver, you should visit International Falls on the Canadian border. Residents of this town, which calls itself the "Ice Box of the Nation," proudly brave some of the lowest temperatures in the country. For indoor fun, the Mall of America in

Bloomington is the most visited shopping mall in the world. It's so big there's an entire amusement park inside!

Minneapolis is one of the country's biggest manufacturing cities, but Minnesota is a farming state as well. Growing grain and producing lots of dairy products earns Minnesota the nickname "The Bread and Butter State." More turkeys are raised here than in any other state, but the big export is iron ore, used in making steel. Two-thirds of America's iron sails across Lake Superior from Minnesota mines.

Split Rock Lighthouse, Lake Superior, Minnesota

North Dakota

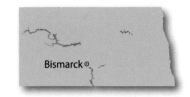

Bismarck ⊙

North Dakota and South Dakota both became states on the same day, but we don't know in what order. President Benjamin Harrison sneakily covered up the names of the states on the admission papers, shuffled them up, and then signed them!

The twin Dakotas have a lot in common— they both have very small populations within a very large area, and they are the top two states in relying on agriculture for their economy. The average farm in North Dakota is well over 1,000 acres, and in its short growing season North Dakota produces more wheat than any other state except Kansas. Then it's time to hunker down for a long, cold winter!

It's too dry for farming in the western part of the state, so cattle and sheep are raised instead. Temperatures can range from 120 degrees Fahrenheit in the short summers to -60 degrees Fahrenheit in their bitterly cold winters, yet farmers and ranchers have adapted, or found ways to adjust, to the extreme climate.

There are several Native American reservations in North Dakota; ***Sacagawea***, Lewis and Clark's Shoshone guide, was from this state. Born in Idaho, as a young girl she was taken prisoner by another warring tribe, who made her their slave and took her to North Dakota. Some years later, Lewis and Clark met Sacagawea, now a young woman, and arranged to take her with them as an ***interpreter*** among the many different tribes whom they would meet on their explorations. (An interpreter is one who is able to speak two or more languages and is able to help people who speak different languages understand one another.) On this journey of exploration, Sacagawea walked thousands of miles, from North Dakota to the Pacific Ocean and back again, carrying her baby on her back. North Dakota's largest man-made lake, located entirely in one state, is named for this remarkable woman.

North Dakota shares its northern border with Canada; the friendship between our two nations is symbolized by the beautiful International Peace Gardens near the border.

Lewis and Clark with Sacagawea, by Charles Russell

South Dakota

The Missouri River cuts straight through the middle of South Dakota. On the mostly flat lands on the east side of the river, huge farms grow corn, wheat, soybeans and alfalfa. On the west side of the river, livestock is raised. Altogether, South Dakota's economy relies on agriculture more than any other state, but it is expanding into other industries.

Mount Rushmore

Wild Bill Hickok, frontiersman

Black Elk, Sioux leader

Wild Bill Hickok, a famed frontiersman; Laura Ingalls Wilder, author of *Little House on the Prairie*; and Black Elk, Sioux leader and convert to Catholicism, are among the famous people of frontier days who are associated with South Dakota. That heritage continues as rodeos and pow-wows are still held here every year.

The Black Hills in the western part of the state are popular with tourists, who camp there and visit the Mount Rushmore National Monument. This monument honors four of our greatest presidents, while the Chief Crazy Horse Memorial which is still under construction will honor Native American heritage— South Dakota has the third largest Native American population in the country. (From a distance, the Black Hills do look black, but as you get closer you'll see they are actually covered with thick pine forests.)

South Dakota's Badlands—so named because of the hardships early travelers faced traveling through them—are now visited by tourists who want to see the strange but beautiful steep rock formations unique to this state's geography.

Student Workbook: Complete pgs. 42-46.

NEBRASKA

IOWA

COLORADO

KANSAS

MISSOURI R.

Platte R.

Missouri R.

Arkansas R.

NEW MEXICO

OKLAHOMA

Oklahoma City ★

ARKANSAS

Little Rock ★

TEXAS

Austin ★

Mexico

INDIANA

OHIO

ILLINOIS

Ohio R.

Lake Erie

PENNSYLVANIA

NEW JERSEY

★ Dover

DELAWARE

Annapolis ★

Washington D.C. ★

MARYLAND

Charleston ★

WEST VIRGINIA

Frankfort ★

KENTUCKY

VIRGINIA

Richmond ★

Nashville ★

TENNESSEE

Raleigh ★

NORTH CAROLINA

Columbia ★

SOUTH CAROLINA

MISSISSIPPI

Atlanta ★

GEORGIA

Montgomery ★

LOUISIANA

Jackson ★

ALABAMA

Baton Rouge ★

Tallahassee ★

FLORIDA

Atlantic Ocean

Bahama Islands

Southern Region

Washington Monument

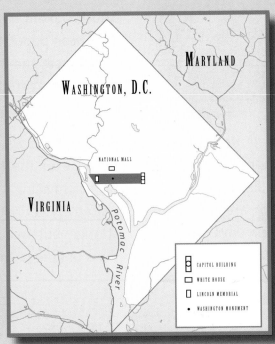

MARYLAND

WASHINGTON, D.C.

NATIONAL MALL

VIRGINIA

Potomac River

☐ CAPITOL BUILDING
☐ WHITE HOUSE
☐ LINCOLN MEMORIAL
• WASHINGTON MONUMENT

Lincoln Memorial

District of Columbia

Part 3

"Settlement of Maryland by Lord Baltimore" by Emanuel Leutze. Courtesy of the Maryland Historical Society, Item ID #1884.2.1.

Florida · Maryland · Virginia · Delaware · Georgia · North Carolina · South Carolina · West Virginia

The Southern Region

Washington, D.C. · Alabama · Kentucky · Mississippi · Tennessee · Louisiana · Texas · Arkansas · Oklahoma

The Southern Region

Being "Southern" unites the people of this region in a way that may seem mysterious to outsiders. No physical boundary separates the North from the South, yet no one would deny that a distinct culture, history, and set of traditions gives the southern states a uniqueness all their own.

The differences between northern and southern states were obvious even in the beginning of American history. These differences grew deeper with each passing year. As time passed, the North grew more industrialized, with an economy that depended on factories, while the South relied more and more on agriculture, or farming. Although slavery was eventually outlawed in the North, the institution of slavery grew stronger in the South because of the need for people to work on huge southern farms, called **plantations**.

Eventually, these differences between states became so great that most of the southern states wanted to **secede** from, or leave, the **Union** (the name for all the states united as one country). The states that seceded, or left the Union, formed the southern **Confederacy**, also called **The Confederate States of America**.

Southern plantation, 1883

"Holding the Line at all Hazards" by William Gilbert Gaul

President Abraham Lincoln did not believe the southern states had a right to leave the Union. He knew that the division, if allowed to occur, would forever break our one nation into two smaller, separate countries! This sad and unfortunate separation led to the *Civil War*, which left most southern states in ruins and changed the South forever.

For four long years, Americans fought Americans. Choosing sides was very difficult for people as important as the president, right down to families like yours and mine. Generals Ulysses Grant and Robert E. Lee were two famous Civil War generals. Grant and Lee both had ties with the North, and also with the South. Both had attended the same northern military college, West Point, and had served in the same army before the Civil War. Both loved their country very much. Grant and Lee had both owned slaves; both freed their slaves. Yet each general chose a different path. In the Civil War, General Grant led the northern Union forces, while General Lee chose to lead the southern Confederate army.

Some families were torn apart forever. Even President Lincoln's family was affected. Mrs. Lincoln was from the South; two of her brothers were killed fighting for the Confederacy. There are also several sad stories about brothers—one who chose to join the Union Army and the other who chose to join the Confederate Army—who wound up fighting against each other in the same battle!

In 1865, the Confederacy **surrendered**, or agreed that they had lost and would stop fighting. In the end, over 650,000 Americans lost their lives—almost as many deaths as every other war in American history combined. Most of the southern states lay in ruins. The slow process of **Reconstruction**, or rebuilding the South, began. The United States was one country again, but the Civil War had changed the South forever.

The most important change brought about by the Civil War was the ending of slavery. During the war, President Lincoln had issued the Emancipation Proclamation, declaring all slaves in the rebelling states to be free. Then, in 1865, Congress passed the Thirteenth Amendment to the Constitution, which made slavery illegal forever.

Slavery was ended, but this did not end all racial conflict. For many years, African-Americans struggled for equality, or their right to enjoy the freedoms that our nation's rule of law, the Constitution, gives to all citizens. However, today African-Americans are regularly elected to high positions in government by people of all races, and southern schools are the best *integrated* (including people of any race) in the country.

Agriculture is still important to the southern economy, but the South now boasts some of America's biggest manufacturing cities. The South is one of the fastest-growing areas in the country, and millions of immigrants and northerners have arrived to add their own twist to southern traditions.

The South is divided into three smaller regions—the South Atlantic region, the East South-Central region, and the West South-Central region.

Student Workbook: Complete pg. 49.

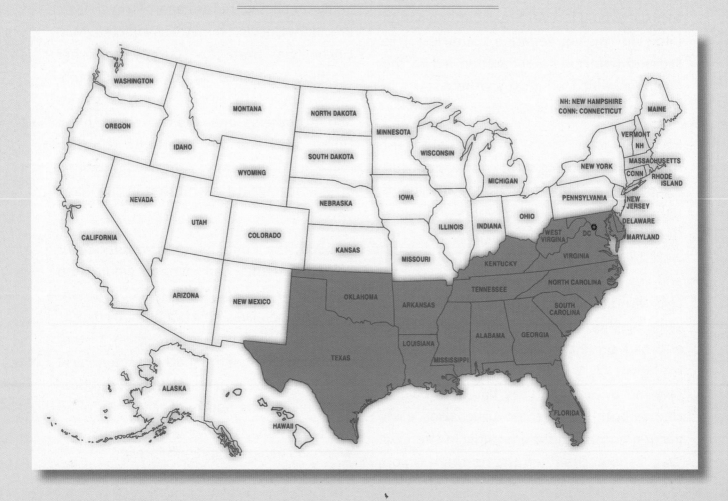

South Atlantic
REGION

The South Atlantic states are: **Florida, Maryland, Virginia, Delaware, Georgia, North Carolina, South Carolina, West Virginia,** and **Washington, District of Columbia** (which is not a state, but the capital of all our United States!).

All the South Atlantic states (except Florida and West Virginia) belonged to the thirteen original colonies. In many ways, this makes these states the "original" South. The imaginary *Mason-Dixon Line*, that you learned of earlier, forms an unofficial border between North and South.

Visitors to the southern Atlantic coast are greeted by sandy beaches and hundreds of little islands to explore. The flat Atlantic coastal plain provides plenty of excellent farmland, with rolling rivers and murky swamps filling the landscape. Some of the best soil in the country is found here. The region extends westward to the Piedmont—the gentle foothills of the *Appalachian Mountains*.

Because of the region's rich soil, agriculture has been the most important part of this region's economy from the beginning. It still is, but huge cities like Atlanta, Georgia have a modern flair, and the Kennedy Space Center in Florida is the launch site for America's astronauts! Washington, D.C., our nation's capital, is also found in this region—our country's biggest decisions are made here. The people of the South Atlantic states respect their past while helping build the future.

South Atlantic summers are long, hot, and humid, but winters are mild. If you come for a visit, do expect plenty of rain—at least some falls every month.

Turn to LESSONS ALIVE! on pgs. 47-48 of your workbook for enrichment activities.

Florida

Maryland

Virginia

Delaware

Georgia

North Carolina

South Carolina

West Virginia

Washington D.C.

Florida

Tallahassee

Although he explored the New World for other reasons, Spanish explorer *Juan Ponce de León* may also have been searching for the mythical Fountain of Youth—a magical spring to keep him alive forever! Why didn't he realize that we already have the secret of Eternal Life? After all, he named the land he was exploring *Pascua Florida*—the Spanish name for the Easter season.

The Spanish founded the city of *St. Augustine* (named for the great Doctor of the Church) in Florida in 1565. This city still stands as the oldest permanent European settlement in all of North America.

For two hundred years the Spanish ruled Florida. Jesuit priests and Franciscan friars taught local tribes about Jesus and helped maintain peace. African-American slaves from the British colonies often fled to Florida where the Spanish promised them freedom if they became Catholic. Sadly, Florida's role as a haven for freedom did not last, and slavery came to the territory.

England took control of Florida through a treaty in 1763, but then returned it to Spain after the American Revolution. In 1819, the *Adams-Onis Treaty* peacefully settled arguments between the United States and Spain over territory they both claimed. Through this treaty, Spain gave Florida to the United States.

The Seminole tribe resisted American settlement, but the American military forced most of the tribe to move west. Some Seminole escaped into the swamps of southern Florida, where their descendants still live today.

Florida became a state in 1845, but less than 16 years later it seceded from the

Ponce de León searching for the Fountain of Youth

Union to join the Confederacy in the Civil War. Following the war, Florida returned to the Union along with all the other states in the Confederacy, which no longer existed.

Most of Florida is a 450-mile peninsula jutting out of the southeast corner of our nation, making it the most southern state in the continental United States. It is also our lowest and flattest state. Britton Hill, Florida's highest peak, is only 345 feet above sea level!

Florida has more coastline than any other state but Alaska, so in Florida you're never far from the beach. Florida's east coast lies on the Atlantic Ocean, where the sand is hard and thick. On the west coast is the Gulf of Mexico, where the sand is soft and filled with seashells to collect. The northwest part of the state is called the Panhandle. (Why do you think that is? Look at the map and see if you can tell why.) The sand here is glistening white. Off the southern coast you'll find a series of little islands called the Florida Keys.

Much of southern Florida lies within the **Everglades**, one of the largest swamps in the world. The northern part of the swamp has been drained for farming, but the southern part is a huge wildlife preserve. Snakes, turtles, manatees, herons, panthers, and hundreds of other exotic animals live here. Watch out: in Florida, wherever you find freshwater, there's probably an alligator in there somewhere!

With warm weather all year long, "The Sunshine State" attracts vacationers year round. Each year, vacationers spend more than $40 billion, visiting countless amusement parks like Universal Studios and SeaWorld in Orlando, and Walt Disney World, the biggest vacation resort on earth. Did you guess that tourism is Florida's biggest industry?

Florida's warm weather also allows farming of unique crops throughout the whole year. Most of the world's oranges and grapefruits come from Florida, and more sugarcane is grown here than in any other state. (Florida's weather isn't *always* nice. Hurricanes have caused a lot of damage over the years.)

Alligators

John F. Kennedy Space Center

The John F. Kennedy Space Center in Cape Canaveral is where every U.S. manned space flight has been launched since 1968. With 24 military bases in Florida, military work is also a major part of the economy.

For most of its history, Florida had the smallest population in the South. With an incredibly diverse population that is growing faster than that of any other state, Florida is now the fourth most populous state in the country! Nearly two-thirds of the population was born out of state. Almost a quarter of Floridians are Hispanic and a slightly smaller number are African-American. Millions of senior citizens from around the country also come to Florida to retire.

A Nation Built by Immigrants

Senator Marco Rubio

Senator Marco Rubio

In the late 1950s, Cuba's Communist leaders began to persecute Christians and other Cubans who spoke out against the government. A number of these Cubans lost their jobs or were sent to jail for many years. Thousands and thousands then fled Cuba and immigrated to the United States. Can you guess which state most of them immigrated to? (Find Cuba on a world map and see which state is closest to Cuba.)

Today, Florida has the biggest Cuban-American population of any state. One famous Cuban-American is Florida Senator Marco Rubio.

Florida's
Catholic Heritage

Nombre de Dios Mission

"What is that?"

"I don't see anything."

"Look! On the horizon!"

"Oh! I think I see something now."

Maybe these are some of the things members of the Timucua tribe said as the small dots on the ocean grew slowly to the size of huge warships. They had never seen such ships and were afraid, but they were also a proud people. If these strangers wanted a fight, they would get one!

After much waving of flags, firing of cannons, and blowing of trumpets, a fierce-looking European general exited the ship. The Timucua looked on, waiting to see what would happen next. Would the Europeans try to destroy them? Suddenly, it got very quiet, and then . . . another European in a black robe started singing at the top of his lungs! He approached the general and gave him something.

"Is it a weapon?"

"No. It's not a weapon. It's just a piece of wood."

The mighty general and all his soldiers fell to their knees at the sight. The general kissed the piece of wood and the man in the black robe began to speak.

"What is he talking about?"

"I don't think he's talking. He's praying—praying to his God."

The date was September 8th, 1565—Our Lady's birthday, and the day of the founding of St. Augustine, the very first permanent European settlement in the future United States. The fierce-looking general was Pedro Menendez de Aviles of Spain. *Father Francisco Lopez* was the "black robe." The piece of wood was a small wooden cross. When Father Lopez placed that cross in the soil, America's first parish and mission began—the Mission of Nombre de Dios ("the Name of God"). More than four centuries later, the mission is still there for you to visit!

From the very beginning, Nombre de Dios faced many challenges. Twenty-eight priests had left Spain with Father Lopez, but only four survived the dangerous journey across the ocean. Nonetheless, through the grace of God, Father Lopez impressed the native people with his love for God. The Spanish and the Timucua became great friends and soon the whole tribe converted to the Catholic faith.

In the early 1600s, many Spanish people developed a devotion to Our Lady of La Leche. Settlers brought this devotion with them and Nombre de Dios' chapel was dedicated in her honor. This wooden structure was the first shrine dedicated to Our Lady in the United States. Unfortunately, St. Augustine and the mission faced constant attacks from their French and British rivals in the north. During these attacks the shrine was destroyed, but each time the missionaries patiently rebuilt it. Eventually a more permanent chapel was built out of stone. Sadly, during a British attack in 1728, the Spanish destroyed the chapel themselves to prevent it from falling into enemy hands.

With the destruction of the chapel, many thought that Nombre de Dios would disappear. In 1763, Spain gave Florida to England, and most Spanish Catholics fled. Soon, most of the Florida missions were empty and forgotten. In 1776—the same year the United States declared its independence—a group of Catholic survivors of a failed colony settled in St. Augustine, bringing the Faith back. In 1783, Florida was returned to Spain and two dedicated priests arrived to begin restoring the missions.

When Spain gave Florida to the United States in 1819, the Church again flourished in this southern state. Then in 1861, the first shots of the Civil War rang out! St. Augustine was captured by Union (northern) soldiers, but Nombre de Dios did its best to minister to the war-torn city. In 1875, the Chapel of Our Lady of La Leche was finally rebuilt. Even destruction by a hurricane could not conquer this sacred place: the chapel was rebuilt for good in 1914.

Time marched on . . . During World War II many soldiers were sent to St. Augustine for a break from the war. Years later, in the 1960s, terrible race riots burned through the city. Through these violent times, many found comfort within the quiet walls of Nombre de Dios. From the beginning of American history, this simple mission has kept prayerful witness, through good times and bad. As you read this, someone may be finding peace there right now.

Our nation has been through many changes and challenges—but the Name of God has always been with us!

Fr. Francisco Lopez, "Landing at Nombre de Dios" by Stanley Meltzoff

Maryland

Every Catholic in America should study Maryland. Why? Because the colony of Maryland was founded by Catholics! In the 1600s, Catholics in England were persecuted and even killed for their faith, so **King Charles I** created the colony of Maryland. Catholics could move to this new colony to live in safety.

Many books will tell you that Maryland was named for the king's Catholic wife (her name was Henrietta Maria) and there might be some truth in that. However, when the first Catholic colonists landed in Maryland on the Feast of the Assumption, Jesuit priest Father Andrew White dedicated the new colony of Maryland not to the Queen of England, but to the Queen of Heaven—the ever-Virgin Mary, the Mother of God!

Maryland played a key role in the American Revolution. The **Treaty of Paris**, which officially ended the war with Britain in 1783, was signed in Annapolis, the state capital.

Not so many years after the peace treaty was signed, the United States and Britain went to war again! In this **War of 1812**, a lawyer named **Francis Scott Key** was sent on board a British ship to help arrange for captured prisoners to be set free.

While there, he discovered the British were planning to attack Fort McHenry, which protected the port city of Baltimore. He was then held prisoner himself! Stuck on the ship, he could not warn the Americans and was forced to just watch the battle helplessly.

It was a dark night, but through bright flashes of "the rockets' red glare" and "bombs bursting in air," Key kept catching sight of the American flag—this proved the Americans had not been defeated. Key wrote a poem

"By Dawn's Early Light" by Edward Percy Moran

111

Battle of Antietam

called "Defense of Fort McHenry," but we know it better by a different title. Do you know what the title is?*

Slavery was legal in Maryland, but not all Marylanders accepted slavery. In the years after the American Revolution, many plantation owners chose to free their slaves voluntarily, but others did not. By the time of the Civil War, half of the African-Americans in Maryland were free, but half were still slaves. Maryland stayed in the Union, but is sometimes called a **Border State** because it tried not to openly take sides with either the North or the South. Despite this, many battles took place here. More lives were lost in one day at Maryland's **Battle of Antietam** than on any other day of the war.

Maryland is located on the Atlantic coast of our country. Its many rivers flow into the massive Chesapeake Bay, which almost cuts Maryland in half. Most people live along the coastal strip on the western shore. The eastern shore is shared with Delaware and Virginia. This region is sometimes called the Delmarva Peninsula. (Delmarva is a funny word. Is it Spanish? A Native American word? It's neither. DELaware + MARyland + VirginiA. Get it?) No visit to Maryland is complete without seeing the beautiful Blue Ridge Mountains and the famous Allegheny and Potomac Rivers.

Sitting by the ocean, Maryland is often hit with severe weather, such as hurricanes, tornadoes and floods.

It shouldn't be surprising that **Clara Barton**, who founded the **American Red Cross** to help people in need from natural and other disasters, was a Maryland native. (Why do you think a symbol for helping the suffering is a red cross?)

Agriculture has always been a big part of Maryland's economy. Corn and soybeans are major crops, and tobacco has been grown in Maryland since colonial times. Poultry and dairy products are also part of Maryland's agricultural production. Coal mining provides jobs along a narrow piece of land on the western shore where the Appalachian Mountains cross Maryland.

Maryland is best known for its fishing industry. Millions of pounds of seafood are caught in the Chesapeake Bay every year—some people think Maryland crabs are the best in the world. Besides being a center of the fishing industry, the city of Baltimore is one of America's most important shipping ports.

Food products, communication equipment, and steel products are manufactured in Maryland, but the biggest employer is the **federal** government. Our country's capital and home of our nation's government, Washington, D.C., is so close that many people drive to work here from their homes in Maryland every day.

Oh! thus be it ever, when freemen shall stand
    Between their loved home and the war's desolation!
Blest with victory and peace, may the heav'n-rescued land
    Praise the Power that hath made and preserved us a nation.
Then conquer we must, when our cause it is just,
And this be our motto: "In God is our trust."
    And the star-spangled banner in triumph shall wave
    O'er the land of the free and the home of the brave!
—Final stanza of "The Star-Spangled Banner" by Francis Scott Key

Maryland's Catholic Heritage

The Story of Charles Carroll

In the early 1600s, **George Calvert** had an important job working for the king of England, but when he became a Catholic he faced a problem. Catholics weren't allowed to work for the king without giving up their religion. George Calvert refused to do this. He lost his job, but the king gave him some land in America as a gift for his years of good work. This was the beginning of Maryland.

Catholics in Maryland remembered how cruelly they had been treated in England. Has anyone ever treated you in a mean way? Did you want to be mean back to them? The Calvert family owned Maryland and could make any rules they wanted. They could have **banned** non-Catholics from their colony—that is, made a law forbidding them to enter—but instead they invited them in. They also could have been as cruel to non-Catholics as they had been to them, but they knew that was wrong. Jesus tells us to love our enemies. A special law, *The Toleration Act of Maryland*, declared that all Christians—Catholic and non-Catholic—had to be treated equally.

The Toleration Act did not bring the happy ending it might have. Religious fighting continued in England. In 1688, Catholic King James II was forced from power by William of Orange, a Protestant. After that, things started to get worse for Catholics all over the British Empire—which included the colony of Maryland. The power to rule was taken away from the Calverts. Catholics were no longer allowed to be leaders or lawyers. Worse still, public Mass was forbidden, and parents were not even allowed to teach the Faith to their children! Finally, in 1718, Catholics lost the right to vote.

Because of these cruel laws many Catholics moved away from Maryland, but **Charles Carroll** did the opposite. He moved to Maryland from Ireland—where Catholics were also suffering greatly under the British. Carroll became a respected lawyer in Maryland, rising to Attorney General of the whole colony. This was just before Catholics were banned from important positions. When that happened, Carroll was forced to give up being a lawyer. He was even thrown in jail twice for speaking his mind!

Carroll wanted to help his colony, but because he was a Catholic he wasn't allowed to. He loved Maryland, and didn't want to leave. Instead, he bought some land and became a farmer. He was so successful that when he died he was the richest man in the colony.

This wasn't the end of the Carroll family. Despite persecution, three of Charles' grandsons would go on to make history. This is one of their stories. (See if you can find the other two Carrolls "hidden" in different sections of this book.)

Before the American Revolution, **Charles Carroll of Carrollton** (Charles Carroll the Settler's first grandson) believed the American colonies needed to become independent from England. It's hard to believe now, but most people didn't feel that way at the time. Even though Carroll had good ideas, no one wanted to hear them because he was Catholic.

Around this time, a mysterious person who signed his name "First Citizen" started writing articles about independence in the newspaper. Another man started writing articles saying

independence was a bad idea. These articles were very popular and most people agreed "First Citizen" made a better argument. People started to believe that independence from England was a good idea. Everyone wanted to know who "First Citizen" really was. I'm sure you've already guessed: "First Citizen" was Charles Carroll! Many people who wouldn't listen to Carroll just because he was Catholic were sorry.

Carroll became such a famous voice for independence that he was chosen to represent Maryland as a **delegate** at the meeting where the **Declaration of Independence** was written and signed. (Did you remember that a delegate is a person chosen to represent and speak for a larger group of people?) The only Catholic signer, Carroll made a great impact on the other delegates. They started to wonder whether Catholics were really so bad.

Years later, some of these same men wrote the Constitution and the Bill of Rights, which is a set of amendments (changes) to the Constitution that protect our most important freedoms. The First Amendment protects the right to freely practice any religion one wants. Millions have come to America for that promise in the First Amendment—perhaps written in honor of that surprising Catholic, Charles Carroll of Carrollton.

SOUTHERN REGION — SOUTH ATLANTIC

Mysteries of History *Look! It's a Clue!*

"Why are those children traveling to school on a ship?"

Let's find out!

Imagine that you were a child growing up in Maryland in the late 1600s. If parents wanted their children to go to a Catholic school, the children didn't take a school bus to get there, but rather a ship! Can you guess why?

As you now know, for many years it was illegal to celebrate Mass in public in the colony of Maryland. Church property was destroyed and priests driven out. Only one priest was able to stay in the whole colony, and he had to hide! Catholic schools were illegal, so to attend Catholic school, children took a ship and sailed all the way across the Atlantic Ocean to France.

Can you imagine leaving your family for a year or more, to go to school in a foreign land, with teachers who did not speak your language?

Yet, for love of God and their Holy Faith, that is just what some children did.

"Charles Carroll of Carrollton" by Thomas Sully

"Without morals, a republic cannot subsist any length of time; they therefore who are decrying the Christian religion . . . are undermining the solid foundation of morals, the best security for the duration of free governments."

Charles Carroll of Carrollton

Virginia

In 1584, British Queen Elizabeth I sent explorer **Sir Walter Raleigh** to claim land in the New World for England, before France and Spain grabbed it all. Elizabeth was nicknamed "the Virgin Queen," so these lands became known as Virginia. Raleigh's colony of **Roanoke** (in modern day North Carolina) was the first English settlement in North America. After a few years, a ship came from England to visit the little colony, but all the people of Roanoke had mysteriously disappeared! To this day, we don't know how or why. Maybe one day you will solve this mystery.

In 1607, the first permanent English settlement of **Jamestown** was founded on a little peninsula on the James River. These first 100 settlers had a hard time at first. Many died of starvation, and conflict with the Powhatan tribe cost many lives. If Powhatan princess **Pocahontas** had not begged that the life of colony leader **Captain John Smith** be spared, it is possible the Powhatan would have wiped all the English out. Peace between the Powhatan tribe and the colonists returned but, unfortunately, the peace lasted only a short time. After years of violence on both sides, the British army put down most Native American resistance.

Around this time, a new group of people began to arrive—but not by choice. Thousands of African slaves were shipped to Virginia and forced to labor on large tobacco plantations.

During the American Revolution, many Virginians were inspired to join in the fight by Governor **Patrick Henry's** rallying cry, "Give me liberty or give me death!" And a good thing too! The

"Patrick Henry Before the Virginia House of Burgesses" by Peter F. Rothermel

117

Mount Vernon, the home of George Washington

General Robert E. Lee at Fredericksburg, Virginia

British surrender at Yorktown, Virginia, ended the war, winning independence for a new nation.

Seven of our first twelve presidents were Virginians. (An eighth Virginian, Woodrow Wilson, would be elected in 1912.) Before he led his country to victory, **George Washington** lived as a wealthy planter at Mount Vernon, Virginia, but you probably know him best as our country's very first president.

Thomas Jefferson, author of the Declaration of Independence and our third president, designed his own home of Monticello. Montpelier was the home of President James Madison, the "Father of the Constitution." These presidential homes are now national landmarks that you can visit in Virginia.

During the Civil War, Richmond, the capital of Virginia, became the capital of the whole Confederacy. More battles were fought in Virginia than anywhere else, and the war also officially ended here, when the Confederacy surrendered at Appomattox. Virginian **General Robert E. Lee** gallantly led the Confederate Army through this bloody war. Arlington National Cemetery, located on the land where Robert E. Lee once lived, honors soldiers from every American conflict.

Blue Ridge Mountains

The Civil War changed Virginia forever. The end of slavery also ended the large plantation system, so Virginia began to add more variety to its economy. Tobacco is still grown, but so are lots of other crops, like peanuts, corn, and sweet potatoes. Poultry and hogs are also raised here. Coal is mined in the western part of the state, and the trees of Virginia's forests are used to make paper and furniture. Clothing and food processing are big businesses today, and Virginia is also a leader in computer technology. Most of the region's shipping is done from the port of Hampton Roads, and the city of Newport News builds warships for the navy.

The fastest growing industry in Virginia today is the federal, or national, government! More than 23,000 people work in the **Pentagon**, the headquarters of the United States Department of Defense and one of the largest office buildings in the world. There are also many military bases throughout the state; Norfolk is the headquarters for the U.S. Navy's Atlantic fleet. Many of those who work for the federal government travel from their homes in Virginia to the federal capital of Washington, D.C., every day.

The Chesapeake Bay separates most of Virginia from a small section on the Delmarva Peninsula. (Do you remember what Delmarva stands for?) On the eastern coast of Virginia is a sandy plain called the Tidewater region; at the southeastern tip is Virginia Beach, one of the most popular beaches in the world. In the western part of Virginia, the lowlands of the Piedmont rise into the Blue Ridge Mountains. (From a distance the ridges do look blue.) For a breathtaking view, drive along Skyline Drive in Shenandoah National Park. Once you've passed through the mountains, you'll reach the Shenandoah Valley and the Cumberland Gap.

The Pentagon

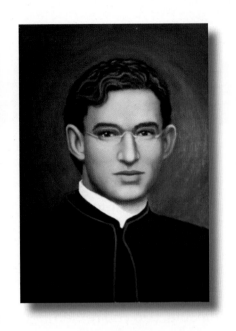

Virginia's Catholic Heritage

The Story of Frank Parater

As Frank Parater laughed and sang around the campfire with the other Boy Scouts, he had a hard time not blurting out his precious secret. His greatest dream had come true: he had been chosen to study for the priesthood in Rome. But that meant leaving his dear friends behind.

At first glance, Frank did not look the outdoors type. Appearances can be deceiving! This small and lanky boy from Richmond, Virginia threw himself into the Boy Scouts from his earliest days. He loved the woods and his fellow Scouts. The other Scouts and leaders were so impressed by this kind-hearted boy that they soon asked him to be a leader himself. He was made the director of the whole Boy Scout camp, which put him in charge of boys much older than himself. All of Richmond was proud the day he became one of the country's first Eagle Scouts—scouting's highest honor.

Outside of scouting, Frank succeeded in almost everything else he attempted—

yet he never bragged or showed off. Many people wondered about the source of his strength and humility. A devout Catholic, he walked to Mass every day. He knew that any success he had in life came from God. "The Sacred Heart never fails those that love Him," became his motto.

His friends and neighbors felt that with Frank's many talents he would grow up to be very successful—he could have any job he wanted and make lots of money. They were stunned when he revealed his true intention of becoming a priest. Serving God meant more to Frank than worldly success.

In 1917, he entered the seminary in North Carolina, where he drew up a Rule of Life for himself that involved daily Communion and devout prayer. Through it all he never forgot his Scouts back in Richmond. Every summer he returned home to the camp to share tales around the campfire and lead them again. It was on the last warm summer night in 1919 that the message arrived—Rome was calling him.

When Frank Parater arrived in Rome, he was eagerly met by Frank Byrne, who was excited to meet another boy from Richmond. The two became fast friends, and Parater quickly earned the same reputation among his fellow students that he had back home. In turn, Parater gave his new friends the greatest compliment he could give. "They are some men here," he said, "regular Scouts."

No one would have imagined that in less than three months the boys would be burying their new friend. Parater suddenly got sick and, eleven days later, he died.

All the joy went out of the college that day. Frank Byrne had the sad task of packing up his friend's belongings. It was then he discovered a letter Parater had written long before he became sick, but labeled not to be opened unless he died. Quickly, Byrne gathered the other boys together and raced to the chapel. He read:

"I have nothing to leave or to give but my life, and this I have consecrated to the Sacred Heart to be used as He wills . . . This is what I live for and in case of death what I die for . . . Death is not unpleasant to me, but the most beautiful and welcome event in life. Death is the messenger of God come to tell us that our novitiate is ended and to

Servant of God Frank Parater

welcome us to the real life . . . I shall not leave my dear ones. I will always be near them and be able to help them more than I can here below. I shall be of more service to my diocese in Heaven than I can ever be on earth."

Suddenly, happiness returned to the boys in the chapel. Frank was right! Death is not the end. Since then, Frank's letter has strengthened popes, clergy, religious, and laypeople during trying times.

There was another letter too. As always, Frank remembered his Scouts back in Richmond. He wrote, "When the time comes for you to hit the trail for home, I'll promise to be near and welcome you to the Campfire of Eternal Life."

Let us pray that we will all be welcomed there someday!

Student Workbook: Complete pgs. 50-53.

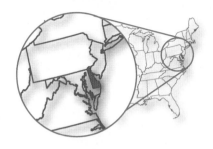

Delaware

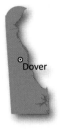

Dover

Originally explored by the English, Delaware was named by Samuel Argall after the governor of the Virginia colony at the time, Lord De La Warr. When Swedish and Dutch settlers came to live here too they did something that many thought was strange. Instead of building their homes out of boards, they made them out of logs—and the log cabin was born!

Delaware proudly earned the nickname "The First State" because it was the first state to sign the Constitution. Even though it was a slave state, Delaware fought on the Union side in the Civil War.

Our second smallest state sits on the Atlantic coast; its fertile plains make great farmland. Visitors love to play on Delaware's beaches or see colonial-era homes, in many of which people still live today. Visitors can also see more than one hundred rooms of colonial artifacts in the Winterthur Museum.

Delaware's laws are great for business; many big companies have their headquarters here. One of these is Du Pont, the largest chemical company on earth, which has given the world Teflon, nylon, polyester, and many other products.

Delaware is also host to one of America's (if not the world's!) most bizarre festivals, the "World National Punkin Chunkin." Slingshots, catapults, and even cannons are brought together for one purpose: to see how far pumpkins can fly! Some pumpkins have been flung more than a mile!

Historic log cabin

Georgia

If you've been following the Appalachian Trail all the way from Maine, you've finally finished your 2,100-mile hike here in Georgia. Are your feet tired yet?

First explored by the Spanish and French in the 1500s, **James Oglethorpe** founded this English colony in honor of King George II in 1733. Sixty years later, **Eli Whitney**

Eli Whitney's cotton gin

invented the **cotton gin**, a machine that made the processing of cotton go much faster. Because of the "gin," much more cotton could be grown and sold. The cotton gin turned cotton-growing into a huge money-maker in Georgia. Unfortunately, millions of African-American slaves were forced to pick more cotton to keep up with the demand for this "cash crop" that was used to make cotton cloth.

Cotton bales

Cotton boll

"Sherman at the Siege of Atlanta," by Thure de Thulstrup

A leader of the Confederacy during the Civil War, Georgia was devastated when Union **General William Sherman**'s troops marched to the city of Atlanta, burning the city to the ground and destroying everything else in their path. Life in Atlanta before and after this event is described in Margaret Mitchell's *Gone with the Wind*, perhaps America's most cherished book. (The movie is great too!) Today, Atlanta has been rebuilt as a major business center, especially for textiles. The great civil rights leader **Martin Luther King, Jr.** was also born in this city.

Don't leave "The Peach State" before you try some peach cobbler. More peanuts are grown here than in any other state, so have some peanut butter pie, too. Now wash it all down with Atlanta's own Coca-Cola!

Supreme Court Justice Clarence Thomas

Clarence Thomas suffered poverty and discrimination growing up in Georgia. Nevertheless, he worked and studied hard. He became a lawyer, and went on to become an associate justice of the Supreme Court of the United States. Justice Thomas is a convert to the Roman Catholic Church.

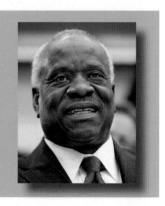

Dr. Martin Luther King, Jr.

After slavery ended, those who had been slaves were recognized by the Constitution to have the same rights as any other citizen of the United States. African-Americans could now own property, live where they wanted, shop where they wanted, and go to school where they wanted. Or could they?

In many places, they could. African-Americans, and people of every race, could live as any other American. But in the South, African-Americans and people of other races as well, were often **discriminated** against, or not allowed the same rights to live as freely as other citizens. Often, children of different races were not allowed to go to school with white children. People of different races might not be allowed to work the same jobs, shop in the same stores, eat in the same restaurants, or even use the same drinking fountains as white citizens.

When Martin Luther King, Jr. was born in Georgia, he faced this type of discrimination. A bright and determined young man, Martin studied hard, graduating high school when he was fifteen years old. He went on to college, became a minister, and a great leader in the Civil Rights Movement, the struggle to end discrimination and bring equal rights to African-Americans. Often, Dr. King was unfairly thrown in jail, but he kept speaking out against injustice. Martin Luther King, Jr. bravely gave his life so that all American citizens could have the same, equal rights.

"I have a dream that one day this nation will rise up and live out the true meaning of its creed: 'We hold these truths to be self-evident; that all men are created equal.' I have a dream that one day on the red hills of Georgia the sons of former slaves and the sons of former slave owners will be able to sit down together at the table of brotherhood.

"I have a dream that my four little children will one day live in a nation where they will not be judged by the color of their skin but by the content of their character." —*from "I Have a Dream," Dr. Martin Luther King, Jr.*

North Carolina

Raleigh

North and South Carolina were once one big colony called Carolina. (It was divided in two in 1729.) In 1562, Jean Ribaut claimed the region for France, naming it for **King Charles IX**. ("Carolus" is Latin for Charles.)

The French never settled here, but the English tried. You remember reading about the lost colony of Roanoke, but in the 1630s and the 1660s two English kings tried again to settle Carolina—this time more successfully. Both of those kings were named Charles, too! Are you surprised they kept the old French name for their colony?

Many battles of the American Revolution took place in North Carolina. Although it was the last state to join the Confederacy in the Civil War, North Carolina provided more troops than any other state. "The Tarheel State" gets its odd nickname from the bravery of its soldiers, who stood their ground as if they had sticky tar on the bottom of their boots!

Tobacco is the state's primary crop, but North Carolina leads all other states in the manufacturing of wooden furniture and textiles, or cloth.

Tobacco field

The western part of the state is famous for the awe-inspiring Blue Ridge and Great Smoky Mountains. In the east, within the narrow islands of the Outer Banks, is Kitty Hawk—where the Wright Brothers successfully flew the world's first airplane in 1903.

"The Wright Brothers" by Ferdinando Tacconi

Columbia

South Carolina

Remember all those kings named Charles? At this point you shouldn't be surprised by what the English called their first town, built in what is now South Carolina. If you guessed Charles Town, you were right! Today we call it Charleston, and it's still a major port just as it was back in 1670.

The Charleston Museum is America's oldest, built in 1773. Many battles in the American Revolution were fought in the state, and South Carolina was the first state to secede from the Union before the Civil War. The first shots of that terrible war rang out when troops from South Carolina attacked Union troops staying at **Fort Sumter** in Charleston Harbor.

The Civil War changed forever a way of life for people who relied on slave labor for their wealth. Today, historic mansions and plantations remind locals and visitors of life before this terrible conflict. Although it is a good thing that slavery was ended, it is unfortunate that many valuable things about Southern culture were also destroyed by the Civil War.

The Blue Ridge Mountains in the west lead into the Piedmont—a hilly plateau. Most manufacturing is done here, especially textiles. Farms in the eastern lowlands grow tobacco, peaches, and soybeans. Myrtle Beach and Hilton Head are popular resorts on the Atlantic Ocean.

Do you have an interest in unusual flowers? South Carolinian Joel Poinsett introduced to the United States a Mexican flower that we often decorate our churches with at Christmas. Can you guess its name?*

A Nation Built by Immigrants

James Hoban

If you could design or draw plans for your very own house, how would you make it special? Would you design a house so huge that you could skateboard or rollerskate in your bedroom? Or would you perhaps include a chapel so Holy Mass could be prayed right in your home?

James Hoban was a gifted architect, or person who designs buildings. He immigrated from Ireland to America not long after the Revolutionary War and settled in South Carolina. Mr. Hoban designed America's most famous house, the White House! In addition to designing the White House, he also had a part in starting America's very first Catholic college, now known as Georgetown University.

The White House

*Answer: The Poinsettia

"View of Fort Sumter, South Carolina" by Conrad Chapman

Mysteries of History *Look! It's a Clue!*

Why are American soldiers shooting at American soldiers at Fort Sumter?

Let's find out!

Before 1860, Americans in the southern states and northern states all thought of themselves as Americans. But in November of 1860, America elected **Abraham Lincoln** to be president. Whether it was true or not, people in the southern states thought President Lincoln cared only about northern states. His election was the last straw for the southern states and, the very next month, southern states began to secede from, or no longer be part of, the Union. South Carolina was the first state to secede.

By April 1861, six more states had said they would no longer "belong" to the United States. But on a little island in a South Carolina harbor sat Union troops from the North. These Northern troops based at **Fort Sumter** were now cut off from the rest of the Union, a tiny island of Northerners all alone in the South.

"The Rescue of the Colors, Battle of Fair Oaks, Virginia" by William Brooke Thomas Trego

The Southerners didn't want the Northern troops on the island. What if the Union troops decided that they wouldn't let ships travel to and from Charleston? You can see why the Southerners didn't want Northern soldiers right there in the middle of the harbor.

Soon the food supplies at Fort Sumter ran low. Would the Union soldiers be left to starve to death on their island? What would the Northern soldiers do?

President Lincoln thought long and hard. He did not want to start a war. But he wouldn't let the Union troops go without supplies. President Lincoln decided to send a supply ship to Fort Sumter. When the Confederate, or Southern, troops heard that the ship was coming, they asked the Union commander to surrender, or give up his position at Fort Sumter.

The commander refused to surrender, so Confederate soldiers began shooting at the fort. Southern Americans and Northern Americans were now fighting against one another, in what became the first battle of America's bloody Civil War.

With these clues, what more can you find out about the Confederate States of America and the Civil War? Grab your detective hat and see what you can discover!

West Virginia

Charleston

Coal mining has always been a major industry and the state is still a top producer of coal. Most people in West Virginia live in rural areas, so most manufacturing takes place in the capital city of Charleston. Chemicals, steel, and glass are made here.

West Virginia's western border is the Ohio River, which businesses use to ship their goods to other states. West Virginia is filled with outdoor adventure. White-water rafting is a thrilling sport, not for the faint of heart! For a calmer activity, relax at one of the state's mineral springs. Ride an 1890s coal car at the Beckley Exhibition Mine, or an old-fashioned train on the Cass Scenic Railroad. Harpers Ferry was the site of **John Brown's Raid**—a violent attempt to steal weapons in order to free slaves in 1859. This bloody raid is considered one of the many causes of the Civil War.

After the attack on Fort Sumter, the country was torn by Civil War. When Virginia joined the Confederacy, the counties in the western part of the state voted to stay with the Union! In 1863, these western counties became West Virginia, which has remained a separate state ever since. "The Mountain State" is the only state that lies entirely in the Appalachian Mountains and the Allegheny Plateau. There is practically no flat land at all, which makes farming very difficult.

Martin Robinson Delany, Civil War Surgeon

Dr. Martin Delany, born in West Virginia in 1812, was one of the first African-American doctors to train at Harvard University, and the first to become a major in the Army. Before the Civil War, Dr. Delany helped slaves escape from the South to freedom in the North. During the Civil War, he served bravely as a doctor to Union troops.

Washington, D.C.

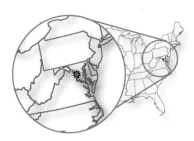

Washington, D.C., is neither a state nor in a state. The Framers of the Constitution worried that when states argued with each other, the state that controlled the capital city would have an unfair advantage. So, it was decided that a special, separate district should be created. President George Washington chose the site between Maryland and Virginia, and dubbed the small piece of land the "District of Columbia." Much of the land was donated by Daniel Carroll—one of only two Catholics to sign the Constitution. The mosquito-filled swamp seemed like an odd choice for the nation's capital, but as the murky waters were drained a city called Washington slowly grew to fill the entire district. Today, the borders of the city and the district are identical, which is why we now call it Washington, D.C.

All three branches of our national, or **federal**, government are headquartered here: **Congress** meets in the Capitol Building, the **president** lives in the White House, and the **Supreme Court** meets in the Supreme Court Building.

When British millionaire James Smithson died, he left lots of money for Washington, D.C., to build the Smithsonian Institution—a series of museums now filled with countless wonders like ancient fossils, rocks from outer space, beautiful artwork, historic artifacts, and even a zoo! The generous Smithson had never been to America, so why did he give our country such an amazing gift? No one knows. It's another mystery of history.

U.S. Capitol Building

Student Workbook: Complete pgs. 54-56.

Lena Frances Edwards, M.D.

Lena Edwards was born in Washington, D.C., in 1900. One of the first African-American women doctors and surgeons, she spoke out in support of unborn children and their mothers, and spent most of her life—and her life savings—caring for the poor. A devout Catholic who attended Holy Mass daily, she was also a Third Order Secular Franciscan. In 1964, Dr. Edwards was honored with the Presidential Medal of Freedom.

Alabama

Kentucky

Mississippi

Tennessee

East South-Central
REGION

The East South-Central states are: **Alabama, Kentucky, Mississippi**, and **Tennessee**.

The East South-Central region could be called America's "first frontier." *Daniel Boone*, a frontiersman in early American history, couldn't resist a challenge, and in his time there was none greater than the impassable *Appalachian Mountains*. When Boone blazed a trail through the *Cumberland Gap* in 1775, he created a safe way through these rugged peaks. Millions of settlers followed him through this famous "gap" to the beautiful and unknown lands on the other side.

These new territories became some of the first states to join the Union after the Thirteen Colonies. The sturdy first settlers and their descendants have added greatly to American culture—especially in their music. Whether you like the blues or bluegrass, country or rock and roll, all these forms of music began here.

Besides the mountains, water helps define this region. The Ohio River forms the region's northern border and the Gulf of Mexico forms its southern border. To the west is the Mississippi River—a blessing for farming, trade, and travel, but also the source of deadly floods in some parts of the region. (Can you trace, with your finger on the map, these important waterways?) In between these powerful bodies of water are many smaller streams and wetlands.

Short, mild winters make way to long, hot, and humid summers. Plenty of rain falls all year long.

Turn to **LESSONS ALIVE!** on pg. 57 of your workbook for enrichment activities.

Alabama

Spanish explorer **Hernando de Soto** travelled through Alabama in 1540, but it was the French who founded the first permanent European settlement in Alabama in 1702. The land was then taken by the British during the French and Indian War in 1763, before being reclaimed by the Spanish again. Spain and the United States would argue over Alabama until the United States eventually gained full control by 1814. Statehood was granted in 1819. All during this "back and forth" for ownership of the land, Native American tribes were caught in the middle. In the 1830s, most of the remaining Native Americans were forced to walk to reservations in far-off Oklahoma and Kansas. Thousands died along this *"Trail of Tears."*

The Black Belt, a cotton-growing region, stretches horizontally across Alabama

In the middle of the state, the rich, black soil of the "Black Belt" is perfect for growing cotton. Thousands of enslaved African-Americans once worked here on huge cotton plantations owned by a few wealthy landowners. These landowners led Alabama to secede from the Union in 1861. The Confederacy's government was first formed in Montgomery, Alabama's capital. Alabama remained an important southern leader throughout the Civil War, earning it the nickname "The Heart of Dixie." When the Confederacy was defeated, Alabama officially returned to the United States in 1868.

"Choctaw Village" by Francois Bernard

Northern Alabama is marked by the hilly **Cumberland Plateau** and the **Appalachian Mountains**. The Tennessee River curves west across the top of the state, but most of the other rivers flow southwest all the way to the Gulf of Mexico.

The Alabama River, which begins as the Coosa River and flows into the Gulf of Mexico, cuts southwest across the state. Follow the river south of the Black Belt into flat plains of equally good soil: Most of Alabama's farms are located here. Your journey ends at Mobile Bay on the Gulf of Mexico. Here you can swim, fish, build sand castles in the white sand, or just watch the ships that come in from all over the world to do business.

In the 1800s and early 1900s, "The Cotton State" relied almost completely on that one crop for its economy. Then, in the 1920s, a tiny insect called the **boll weevil** caused a big problem. Only six millimeters long, this insect killed most of the cotton. Now what would people do to make a living for their families?

A genius named **George Washington Carver** found ways for Alabama farmers to grow other crops through his experiments with peanuts, soybeans, and sweet potatoes. (The next time you eat peanut butter, think of Carver. He invented it!) A former slave, Carver helped save the region that once held him in chains.

Alabama farmers also raise chickens, livestock, and pond-raised catfish. Growing lots of different crops and raising animals has made Alabama farmers even more successful than when they just relied on cotton. Can you believe that there is now a monument honoring the boll weevil in Enterprise, Alabama? (Why do you think that is?)

George Washington Carver

Rosa Parks being fingerprinted by the police

Alabama is also one of the most important industrial states in the South. Alabama's natural resources include coal, limestone, and iron ore for miners to dig. Birmingham, Alabama's largest city, produces so much steel it is nicknamed "The Pittsburgh of the South." (Why is that?*) Huntsville is home to many high-tech industries, including businesses involved in space exploration. Would you like to live the life of an astronaut for a few days? At U.S. Space Camp, located in Huntsville, Alabama, you can!

More than 25% of Alabamans are African-American. In the 1950s and 1960s the state was at the center of the **Civil Rights Movement**, the struggle to bring equal rights to African-Americans. It is sad to know there were once laws separating people because of the color of their skin. In 1955, **Rosa Parks** was arrested when she refused to give up her seat on a bus to a white person. The protests that followed led to the end of that unfair law.

In 1936, German dictator Adolf Hitler organized the summer Olympics thinking he could "prove" that white people were superior to, or better than, people of other races. African-American track star and Alabama hero **Jesse Owens** came home with four gold medals—more than any other athlete. He proved the *real* truth—no one should be judged by the color of his skin.

Sometimes people with disabilities are victims of prejudice too. **Helen Keller**, from Tuscumbia, went blind and deaf as a baby. With the help of her teacher, Anne Sullivan, she learned to communicate, graduated from college, and became a famous author.

*Answer: Pittsburgh, Pennsylvania is known as the "Steel City" because it is the center of the U.S. steel industry.

Jesse Owens

Helen Keller

Alabama's
Catholic Heritage

The Story of Mother Angelica

When Mother Angelica started converting an old garage at the back of her monastery in Irondale, Alabama into a television studio, many people laughed. "What does a **cloistered** nun know about running a television studio?" they would ask. (A cloistered nun lives a private, prayerful life, rarely or never going outside the convent walls.) The feisty nun would be the first to answer: Absolutely nothing! As usual, Mother Angelica wasn't relying on her own abilities, but trusting in Divine Providence.

As a teenager in Canton, Ohio, Mother Angelica once promised God that if she were healed of a terrible illness, she would spread His Word to everyone she could. She was healed, and thought writing books was the way God wanted her to fulfill her promise. By 1976 she had written over 50 books!

It was another promise to God that led her to Alabama. A terrible accident

meant she would probably be paralyzed for life. Her only chance was a risky operation. The night before the operation she promised God if He would allow her to walk again she would build a monastery for His glory in the South. Again she was healed and again, she kept her promise.

Mother Angelica kept writing her books in Alabama, and started making audio recordings of speeches. One day, she was asked if she would like to make a TV show about Catholic teachings for a local television station. She thought it was a strange idea, but she agreed. When she first set foot into the recording studio she thought again about her promise as a teenager. She was pleased to write books, but could television be used to truly fulfill her promise?

Could television be used to spread the Faith? Mother Angelica was determined to find out. From her little studio at the monastery, she continued to film her program for the local station. Unfortunately, the people who ran the station also showed programs that sent bad messages. Mother Angelica saw that television is a powerful tool that must be used responsibly. It can be used for evil or good. Why not use it only for good?

With this idea in mind, Mother Angelica came up with her most ambitious idea—an entire television channel dedicated to Catholic programming and Catholic teaching. Faith in Divine Providence was her only guide.

On August 15, 1981, the Eternal Word Television Network broadcast its first program. At first the network only broadcast for four hours a day; it was hard to find Catholic programs to fill the rest of the day. Mother Angelica was frequently seen teaching and answering phone calls from a small, but growing, number of viewers. Despite many setbacks and through Mother Angelica's tireless leadership, EWTN started broadcasting 24 hours a day in 1987. The people who had laughed at Mother Angelica's idea before were amazed.

Mother Angelica did not stop with this success. Not everyone in the world has a television, so in 1989 she established WEWN (Worldwide Eternal Word Network) to broadcast Catholic programs over the radio. She promised Pope John Paul II that she would use radio to transmit Catholic teaching even into countries where the Catholic Church is illegal.

Pope John Paul II had a special love for Mother Angelica. Once, His Holiness unexpectedly spotted her while passing through a crowd of 5,000 people. He stopped, held her head in his hands and with a big grin said, "Mother Angelica! The Big Chief!" He later told her simply, "Keep doing what you're doing."

Mother Angelica followed the Holy Father's advice and then some. Today, EWTN is the world's largest religious media network, transmitting Catholic programming to 127 countries and almost 150 million homes. EWTN Internet Online Services uses the internet to further Mother Angelica's original mission. Every new technology is another opportunity to bring the Faith to more people.

Mother Angelica is retired now. She spends several hours each day in adoration of the Blessed Sacrament. *Time* magazine once called her "the most influential Roman Catholic woman in America." Even today, as she kneels in silent prayer, she reminds us that any success we have comes only from God's Divine Providence.

Student Workbook: Complete pgs. 58-59.

Kentucky

Frankfort

Kentucky Derby

Do you remember how Daniel Boone conquered America's first unexplored frontier by blazing a trail through the Cumberland Gap in the Appalachian Mountains? The land he found on the other side became known as Kentucky, from a Cherokee word meaning "the land of tomorrow."

After Daniel Boone opened the way, settlers poured into Kentucky, which joined the new country as the 15th state in 1792. Although a slave state, Kentucky remained in the Union during the Civil War. American President **Abraham Lincoln** and Confederate President **Jefferson Davis** were both born in Kentucky—only a hundred miles apart from each other!

Early settlers cleared away the forests of Kentucky for farmland. Today, there are over 87,000 family farms in Kentucky, many of which were started by those early settlers. Major crops are corn, soybeans, tobacco, and wheat. There are also many coal mines in eastern Kentucky.

The Ohio River along Kentucky's northern border helps ship manufactured goods like automobiles, chemicals, and whiskey. The Kentucky Derby horse race spotlights Kentucky's love of horses. Do you like bluegrass music? Come to Kentucky for toe-tapping fun!

The world's largest system of caves can be explored at Mammoth Cave, or perhaps you'd like to stop at the Louisville Slugger Museum, which claims the world's biggest baseball bat. Then there's Fort Knox, which holds 2.5% of all the gold ever refined since the beginning of history. There are so many guards that not even Daniel Boone would be able to get past security!

"Gateway to the West: Daniel Boone Leading the Settlers through the Cumberland Gap, 1775" by David Wright *www.davidwrightart.com*

138

Mississippi

First explored by Spaniard **Hernando de Soto** in 1540, Mississippi moved back and forth between Spanish and French hands for years. Finally, the French lost the area permanently to the English after the French and Indian War in 1763. After the American Revolution, the United States took control, and Mississippi became a state in 1817.

Military graves in the Vicksburg National Cemetery in Vicksburg, Mississippi

As cotton became the most important part of the economy, more and more African slaves were brought in to work on plantations. Today, Mississippi has a higher percentage of African-Americans than any other state, so the state was very important in the Civil Rights Movement.

Mississippi was the second state to join the Confederacy; it suffered the highest percentage of deaths of any state in the Civil War. In response, the first Memorial Day was celebrated here.

Mississippi is named for the mighty river that makes up its western border, where levees (artificial riverbanks) help stop farms from being washed away in floods. Blues music probably started right here in the Mississippi Delta.

Cotton is still a major crop, but Mississippi also leads the nation in tree farming. Farming has always been a big part of Mississippi's economy, but the discovery of oil in the 1930s brought more manufacturing to the state.

When President Teddy Roosevelt refused to shoot a baby bear in the Mississippi woods, Morris Michton honored him with a new toy—the teddy bear!

Anti-Segregation Protest

Tennessee

The Battle of Franklin, Tennessee, 1864

Not everyone who followed the Cumberland Gap followed it all the way to Kentucky. Many liked what they saw in Tennessee, where the Cumberland Gap begins. These pioneers decided to stop and settle here instead, and by 1796 the population was big enough for Tennessee to become the 16th state.

When the federal government asked for 2,800 soldiers during the War of 1812, 30,000 Tennesseans volunteered! Later, many men of the "Volunteer State"— although divided over the Civil War— stayed true to their state's nickname by becoming soldiers for either the Union

or Confederate causes. Eventually, Tennessee, a slave state, became the last state to leave the Union. It would be the first to return after the war.

The Mississippi River forms Tennessee's western border. You'll find the Great Smoky Mountains, America's most visited national park, on the state's eastern side. Tennessee farms grow tobacco and raise cattle, but the mining of natural resources—especially coal and zinc—has always played a big part in the economy. Since the 1930s, the **Tennessee Valley Authority** has helped modernize the eastern part of the state through flood control and by bringing electricity and economic development to the area.

Cumberland coal transport

Tennessee is a land of music: Nashville is the world's country music capital; Beale Street in Memphis is known for the blues; and Graceland was the home of Elvis Presley, "the King of Rock and Roll."

Sequoyah

Do you speak more than one language? If you do, you know that each different language has sounds that are not quite the same as those used in speaking English. The 26-letter alphabet used for reading and writing English works fine for English, but not always so well for the different sounds in different languages.

Born in Tennessee, Sequoyah (George Gist) was a member of the Cherokee tribe. He spoke Cherokee, a language that uses a number of sounds not found in English. Sequoyah wanted to pass down Cherokee history and customs to the children of the tribe. But how could this be done safely if there were no books in the Cherokee language? How could books be written, if there was no Cherokee alphabet?

Sequoyah set to work. It took many years, but by 1821 he had developed a type of "alphabet" with 86 characters, or letters. Each character stood for a different sound in the Cherokee language. Thanks to Sequoyah, the Cherokee people could now write down their history, and their children could read books written in their own language!

Student Workbook: Complete pgs. 60-61.

Louisiana

Texas

Arkansas

Oklahoma

West South-Central
REGION

The West South-Central states are: **Louisiana, Texas, Arkansas,** and **Oklahoma**.

When the great European powers were still struggling for control of North America, this region was in the thick of it. Spanish colonists in Mexico and French colonists in Louisiana both fought for years to control this whole area. Ultimately, France would sell their territories to the United States in the *Louisiana Purchase* of 1803.

Mexico had its own Revolutionary War in which it won independence from Spain. You will read soon the complicated story of how a part of Mexico (called Texas) wound up becoming one of the United States. Meanwhile, the American government gave Native Americans a place to live in Oklahoma, far from settlers. At one point, all of these places were considered "The Wild West"; today the blend of European, Hispanic, and Native American cultures have combined to form a truly special place.

The geography of this region is as diverse as its people. Moving west you'll first find mountains and the Piney Woods forestland. Enjoy the rain in central Texas before you reach the dry Chihuahua desert in the western part of the state. In the northwest you'll even find part of the Great Plains.

Summers are swelteringly hot. The northern parts of this region get snow in the winter, but in the southern parts snow is rare.

Turn to **LESSONS ALIVE!** on pg. 57 of your workbook for enrichment activities.

Baton Rouge

Louisiana

Although the Spanish were the first Europeans to explore Louisiana, they made little attempt to claim the area. In 1682, more than 150 years after these Spanish explorers, **Robert Cavelier de La Salle** claimed Louisiana for France, naming it in honor of French King Louis XIV. La Salle's Louisiana was a massive territory that stretched all the way from the Gulf of Mexico to Canada!

Louisiana Purchase: Ceremony in New Orleans

The city of New Orleans on the Mississippi River quickly became a critical port. When President Thomas Jefferson tried to buy the city for the United States, he was surprised by France's offer to sell the entire Louisiana Territory. For less than 3 cents an acre, the **Louisiana Purchase** of 1803 nearly doubled the size of the United States. Nine years later, the smaller state of Louisiana—named for the once giant territory—was formed. During the Civil War, Louisiana joined the Confederacy, but was defeated by the Union early in the war and returned to the United States.

When the United States bought New Orleans as part of the Louisiana Purchase, it continued to be an important port, becoming the biggest slave-trading center in the South. The city was also the site of the most famous American victory against the British in the War of 1812.

Today, New Orleans is the world's largest bulk cargo port and Louisiana's biggest city. Tourists flock to the city's French Quarter to hear jazz music—a unique American musical form that was born here. Originally played at African-American funerals, jazz music was shared with the whole world by New Orleans musicians like **Louis Armstrong**. New

Louis Armstrong

"Louisiana Bayou 1887" by Joseph Meeker

The Sabine River forms most of Louisiana's western border, with the Mississippi River forming most of the eastern border. The Mississippi River then curves southeast through the rest of the state before emptying into the Gulf of Mexico.

Among Louisiana's many "wetlands" are Lake Pontchartrain, a brackish lake (a mixture of fresh and salt water), and slow-moving streams and marshy wetlands called **bayous**. These low-lying bayous are home to lush vegetation like Spanish moss, as well as muddy-water-loving crayfish, catfish, alligators, and frogs. "The Pelican State" gets its nickname from the odd looking birds that live in these swamps. Louisiana's many waterways make Louisiana the second largest commercial fishing state in the country, supplying the world with 90% of its crayfish and much of its shrimp.

Orleans is also famous for its Mardi Gras (Fat Tuesday) festival, held the day before Lenten fasting begins on Ash Wednesday. This tradition was brought to the city by French Catholics, who settled here more than 200 years ago.

Louisiana sits on the Gulf of Mexico, providing the state with hot and humid summers and short, mild winters. This location also sometimes attracts devastating hurricanes. Hurricane Katrina, our nation's costliest national disaster, struck in 2005, flooding much of New Orleans.

Louisiana is also an important agricultural state. It's our nation's second biggest grower of sweet potatoes and sugar cane, and our third biggest grower of rice. Farmers also grow soybeans and cotton.

Oil and natural gas found here help fuel the world. Once the oil is drilled, Louisiana refineries transform it into usable products. The state is also the country's biggest salt producer.

"The Arrival of the Acadians in Louisiana" by Robert Dafford

Louisiana has a special cultural mix found nowhere else in the country. The early French settlers were called **Creoles**. Today, the term refers to people of mixed European and African heritage, as well as their unique culture. (Almost one third of the population is African-American.) Then in the late 1700s, the Creoles were joined by another group called **Acadians**. These French Catholics were kicked out of Canada by the British and fled to Louisiana. The descendants of the Acadians are called Cajuns. They live mostly in the bayou regions of the state, and many still speak French.

While preserving their own cultures, Creoles and Cajuns have contributed to those of others. Their spicy dishes like gumbo and jambalaya please taste buds all over the world.

A Nation Built by Immigrants

Governor Bobby Jindal

Catholic convert and Louisiana Governor Bobby Jindal became the first descendent of East Indian immigrants to be elected governor of a U.S. state.

Texas

Austin

Austin-based Six Flags amusement park gets its name from the six countries' flags that have all at one time flown over Texas. Try to count them all!

First, there's Spain—although the whole thing was quite an accident. Spanish explorer **Alvar Nuñez Cabeza de Vaca** was the first European to set foot in Texas, but not by choice. In 1528, a shipwreck left him and three of his crewmates stranded there for years!

Spain ignored Texas for over a century after that, until another accident brought France into the picture. In 1685, French explorer **Robert Cavelier de La Salle** attempted to found a settlement at the mouth of the Mississippi River. However, due to inaccurate maps and some navigational errors La Salle accidentally founded his settlement 400 miles further west than he thought— right in Texas.

La Salle's settlement only lasted four years, but it was the beginning of an argument over Texas between Spain and France that would last for over a century. The Spanish responded to French settlement by building a series of Catholic missions in the eastern part of the territory. The French responded

Robert Cavelier de La Salle received in the village of the Caddo Native Americans, 1686, by George Catlin

to these missions by founding more settlements in the southern part.

Over time, the argument only got worse. When France sold a huge parcel of land to the United States in the Louisiana Purchase, they included Texas in the deal. Why not? Since the French government claimed to own Texas, they felt they could sell it to whomever they wished. Of course, an outraged Spain disagreed. In 1819, the United States and Spain signed a treaty formally accepting that Texas belonged to Spain and was not included in the Louisiana Purchase.

Not long afterwards, Spain lost much of its territory in North America: In 1821, Mexico gained its independence from Spain after winning the Mexican War of Independence—and took Texas with it. A new flag was unfurled.

Despite all the arguments over who owned Texas, there were only about 3,500 settlers living in that vast area in 1821. These small settlements were under constant threat from Comanche and other Native American tribes. The new Mexican government thought increasing the settler population might help with this problem, so it created a system in which Americans could claim large parcels of land to form settlements within Texas.

In 1822, **Stephen F. Austin** led 297 Americans to the first of these settlements.

Stephen Austin issuing the title to a tract of land, at his log cabin, 1824, by Henry McArdle

More and more Americans kept streaming in each day. Within ten years, Texas' population had grown to about 40,000 people—almost all Americans.

Some of these Americans felt that Texas should leave Mexico and become its own country. In 1835, a revolution began! At the **Battle of the Alamo,** 200 Texan rebels in an old Spanish mission

The Alamo in San Antonio, Texas

Sketch for "Fall of the Alamo" by Robert Jenkins Onderdonk

Some Texans felt it would be better for their country to become a U.S. state, and in 1845 Texas was annexed by (made a part of) the United States. (Mexico's anger over the loss of Texas was one of the leading causes of the Mexican-American War.) In 1861 Texas, a slave state, joined the Confederacy, before returning to the Union in 1870. (Did you count the flags?)

Our second largest state has a diverse geography. The swamps and piney woods in the east give way to the prairies of central Texas. In the west you'll find deserts and the mountains of the "Big Bend." The Rio Grande is Texas' southwestern border, while the Red River makes up most of the state's northern border. The Gulf of Mexico forms the southeastern border.

fought for 13 days against thousands of Mexican troops. Folk hero *Davy Crockett* and almost all the rebels were killed, but the rallying cry of "Remember the Alamo!" eventually led the Texans to victory. In 1836, the *Republic of Texas* became its own country.

Rio Grande

The country's biggest farms and cattle ranches are in Texas, and the state leads all others in oil production. Dallas is a center for manufacturing and banking. Would you like to visit Houston, which is home to America's largest steelworks as well as the Lyndon B. Johnson Space Center, the control center for all American manned spaceflights?

Or maybe you'd like to see a rodeo, or join in the lively Fiesta San Antonio, which celebrates Texas' rich Hispanic-American culture.

A Nation Built by Immigrants

Archbishop Patrick Flores, First Mexican-American Bishop

As the son of poor migrant workers, young Patrick wasn't even sure he'd be able to stay in school. A kindly bishop stepped in to help, and Patrick was able to finish his education. In time, he was ordained a priest, and later became the first Mexican-American Bishop in the Roman Catholic Church. Some years later, Bishop Patrick Flores was appointed Archbishop of the Archdiocese of San Antonio, Texas.

The Spanns

Texas' Catholic Heritage

The Spanns and the Sweeds

Perhaps this simple rule contains Jesus' most famous words: ". . . whatever you wish that men would do to you, do so to them." (Matt. 7:12) So, who among us would ever choose to be bought and sold as property, forced to work against our will with no chance of freedom? Who would choose to be a slave?

Unfortunately, slavery has existed for so long, no one even knows when it started—in some parts of the world, it continues today. Sadly, you know that our own country was once scarred by this terrible injustice.

When the Mexican government invited Americans to come settle in Texas in the 1820s, it set a few rules too: All property owners must be Catholic, and slavery was strictly forbidden. Many American settlers openly ignored these rules. In 1835, in a little town now called Old Washington, some of these Americans signed the Texas Declaration of Independence—Catholic priests were declared "enemies" and more and more African-American slaves were brought in. By the time Texas became a U.S. state in 1845, there were almost no Catholic churches, but slavery was thriving.

In 1848, the first American Catholics in Old Washington, the Spann family, arrived—bringing 90 slaves of their own (who later took the name Sweed.) You may wonder: how could a Catholic family—who often read the Bible stories of the enslaved Israelites crying out to God for freedom—own slaves themselves? I wish I had an answer for you. We do know the Spanns treated their slaves more kindly than most slave-owners. In particular, they did something that shocked the town.

The Spanns built a small log cabin that became their church. Inside, the Spanns and the Sweeds worshiped together as equals. The Spanns insisted on baptizing their slaves and teaching them about the Catholic faith. (In some southern states, someone caught teaching a slave could be put to death. The laws in Texas were not so strict, but for a slave-owner to educate a slave was almost unheard of.) Now you may wonder: if all the people could be treated equally inside the church, why not outside of it? I wish I had an answer for that too.

When the Union army finally reached Texas on June 19th, 1865 they had an announcement—under the Emancipation Proclamation all slaves in Texas were free! ("Juneteenth" is still celebrated each year in Texas.) Six months later, the 13th Amendment to the Constitution outlawed slavery in the United States forever.

The Civil War left the Spanns bankrupt, without any money. Although the Spanns had lost most of their land, still they gave 100 acres to the Sweeds to live on in peace, to continue worshiping in the Spann chapel with them, as free people.

Unfortunately, freedom did not mean the end of all problems for the Sweeds. Like many African-Americans at this time, they still faced racial prejudice and discrimination—but through these struggles the Sweeds vowed to hold onto their Catholic faith. The Sweeds often found comfort in the Rosary when they suffered for years at a time without access to a priest.

In the early twentieth century, a hate group called the Ku Klux Klan used violence to terrorize African-Americans. (The KKK has a special hatred for Catholics, too, no matter what their race.) Many times, in order to avoid these murderers, the Sweeds smuggled brave

Blessed Virgin Mary Catholic Church

priests to the chapel, hidden under sheets in the back of wagons.

One day, the Spann chapel where the Sweeds worshiped mysteriously burned down. That didn't stop the Sweeds, who held Holy Mass in a parishioner's house for over 20 years. It was so small most people had to stand outside and look in from a window. Then in 1936, a simple, new chapel was built, but it didn't have clean water or electricity.

Despite these trials, the Sweeds still live on the land that the Spanns gave to their family generations ago, and have refused to let their Catholic faith die. They have stood for the truth that we are all God's children, no matter the color of our skin. (In fact, both Spanns and Sweeds are buried together in the Catholic cemetery.)

In 1995, after saving for years and with the help of Catholics from many races and ethnic groups, the Sweeds built the Blessed Virgin Mary Church—a new house of worship worthy of their ancestors' unwavering faith.

Come visit it sometime—everyone is welcome in God's house!

Arkansas

Little Rock

How do you pronounce Arkansas? In the 1880s, the argument between the state's two senators over "Ar-KAN-sas" or "AR-kan-saw" got so heated that a law was passed to decide the issue once and for all! (It's "AR-kan-saw," by the way.) Part of the confusion stems from French settlers' attempts to translate the name of a Native American tribe into French.

France sold Arkansas to the United States as a part of the Louisiana Purchase, and it became a state in 1836. A slave state, it joined the Confederacy in the Civil War. Arkansas gained national attention when the **Little Rock Nine**, a group of African-American students, was not allowed to attend the high school of their choice. At first, they were turned away because of their race, but President Dwight Eisenhower ordered that they must be allowed to attend the school. The Little Rock Nine became a symbol for the struggle to end school segregation, the separation of people because of their race.

Mountain Fork River Valley, Ouachita National Forest

The northern and western parts of the state are called the Highlands—where the Ozark and Ouachita mountain ranges rise. The southern and eastern parts of the state form the Lowlands—a flatter area with rich farmland. Over one-third of the country's rice is grown here, and more broiler chickens are raised on Arkansas farms than in any other state. The most important industry is processing all the food grown on these local farms.

Would you like to dig for gems in America's only diamond mine at Crater of Diamonds State Park? One man who did found a huge, forty-carat diamond—the largest ever discovered in North America!

One of the Little Rock Nine

152

Oklahoma

You remember that often Native Americans were forced to leave their homes when settlers wanted to move into their territory, but where did they go?

Many Cherokees, Chickasaws, Choctaws, Creeks, and Seminoles died on forced marches ("The Trail of Tears") to Oklahoma. ("Okla humma" is a Choctaw name for all Native American peoples.) Originally, this was to be the land where Native Americans could finally live in peace.

The American government promised this land to Native Americans for "as long as the grass grows and the water flows." This promise was broken on April 22nd, 1889, the day American settlers were told they could cross the border and stake land claims.

Settlers rushed in and Oklahoma became a state in 1907. Regardless, Oklahoma still has more Native Americans than any other state except California; almost 10% of the population belongs to the 67 tribes who live here. These tribes still add much to the culture of the state.

In the 1930s, that fierce drought called the Dust Bowl dried up the soil and destroyed many farms. Today, however, farmers grow wheat and raise cattle. Oil and natural gas are the most important industries.

The National Finals Rodeo in Tulsa celebrates roping-and-riding cowboy culture. Would you like to enter the World Cow Chip Throwing Championship in Beaver? It's exactly what you think it is!

Student Workbook: Complete pgs. 62-66.

A Native American encampment, by Jules Tavernier

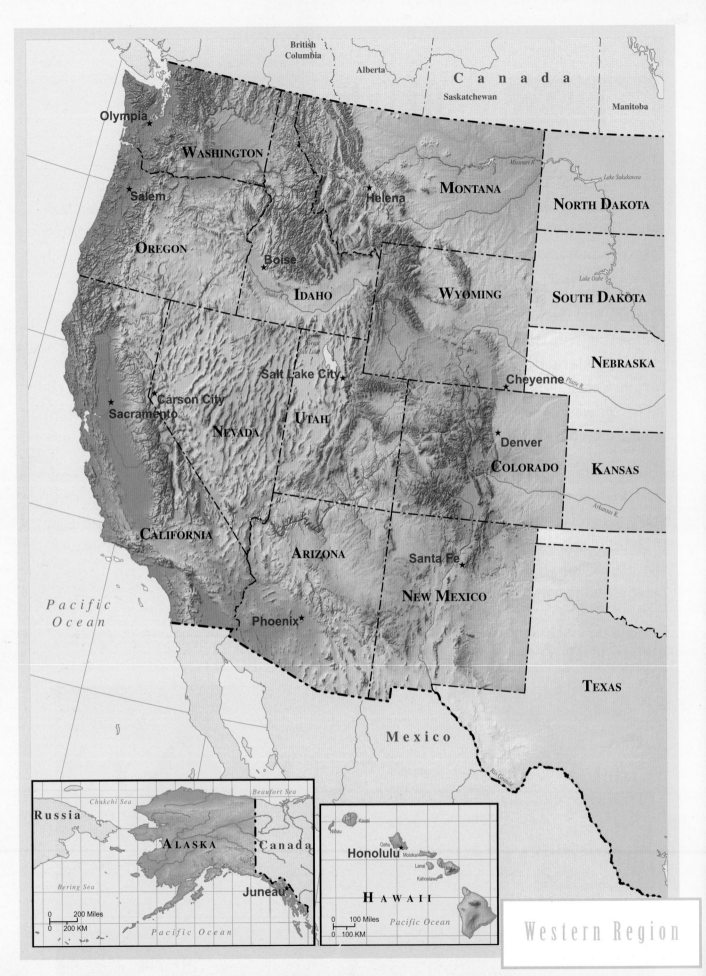

Olympia

WASHINGTON

Salem

OREGON

Helena

MONTANA

British Columbia

Alberta

CANADA

Saskatchewan

Manitoba

NORTH DAKOTA

Missouri R.

Lake Sakakawea

Boise

IDAHO

Snake R.

WYOMING

SOUTH DAKOTA

Lake Oahe

Great Salt Lake

Salt Lake City

UTAH

NEBRASKA

Cheyenne

Platte R.

Carson City

Sacramento

NEVADA

Denver

COLORADO

KANSAS

CALIFORNIA

ARIZONA

Santa Fe

Phoenix

NEW MEXICO

Arkansas R.

Pacific Ocean

TEXAS

Mexico

Rio Grande

Russia

Chukchi Sea

Beaufort Sea

ALASKA

Canada

Kauai

Niihau

Oahu

Molokai

Honolulu

Bering Sea

Juneau

Lanai

Kahoolawe

Maui

HAWAII

Hawaii

Pacific Ocean

0   200 Miles
0   200 KM

0   100 Miles
0   100 KM

Pacific Ocean

Western Region

154

Explorers Lewis and Clark with their guide, Sacagawea, by Edgar Paxson

Part 4

Colorado · New Mexico · Arizona · Idaho · Montana · Nevada · Utah

The Western Region

Wyoming · Alaska · California · Hawaii · Oregon · Washington · U.S. Territories

The Western Region

Perhaps the region with the most extreme geography and climates in America is the West. It's the only region in the country where you can ski on snowy mountains and surf ocean waves in the very same day! In the West, you can climb the nation's highest mountain, and then drop down to its lowest point. This region also boasts of the wettest spot in the country—and the driest.

Both the largest and the oldest living things in the world are found here. Fiery volcanoes sit among frozen tundra; endless forests and huge farms give way to hostile deserts and jagged mountains.

The people of the West have always been just as extreme as its geography. Even today, tales of the 19th-century "Old West" hold a special place in the American imagination. The modern West holds onto much of its pioneer and cowboy heritage, while also adding much more. Ranching, farming, and mining industries are now joined by businesses developing cutting-edge technology and much of the world's entertainment.

Large stretches of uninhabited land between cities give the West the lowest population density in the country, yet it is also the fastest growing region. Immigrants from Latin America and Asia have helped make the West the most ethnically diverse region in the country.

The West is divided into two smaller regions—the Mountain region and the Pacific region.

Mountain
REGION

Colorado

The Mountain states are: **Colorado, New Mexico, Arizona, Idaho, Montana, Nevada, Utah,** and **Wyoming.**

New Mexico

There is no better name for America's highest states than the Mountain region. This area is crowned by the great Rocky Mountains, which run north to south through most of these states; a number of other mountain ranges are scattered throughout the rest of the region.

Arizona

On the eastern side of the Rocky Mountains are the Great Plains. To the west is the Colorado Plateau, filled with awe-inspiring *canyons*, which are deep, narrow valleys with cliffs towering high above. Harsh deserts are found south of the Plateau, yet Native American tribes like the Zuni and Hopi have called this extreme desert environment home for many centuries.

Idaho

In the 1600s, explorers from Spain staked claim to much of this region, pushing out many of the native peoples. After the Mexican War of Independence, this land became a part of Mexico. Then, in the 1820s, the opening of the Santa Fe Trail brought many Americans into this region. This caused conflicts, leading to the Mexican-American War. In 1848, Mexico lost the war and gave this territory to the United States. At first, American settlement grew slowly, but these mountain states are now our country's fastest-growing region.

Montana

Do you like hot, sunny summers, with very little rain? This is the place for you! (But winter in some places brings enough snow to cover your house!)

Nevada

Turn to **LESSONS ALIVE!** on pgs. 67-68 of your workbook for enrichment activities.

Utah

Wyoming

Colorado

Denver
⊙

In the late 1500s, Spanish explorers encountered many Native Americans along the banks of a great river flowing through the mountainous land; red-colored silt tinted its waters. The Spanish used their word *colorado* (red-colored) to describe the river, which was eventually used to name this whole area.

Although the Spanish staked claim to Colorado, they made little attempt to settle it. In 1803, the United States bought the part of Colorado east of the Rocky Mountains through the Louisiana Purchase.

Did you remember that the territories in the Louisiana Purchase were sold by France, not Spain? Of course, this sale made the Spanish government very angry since they claimed to own Colorado! (As usual, no one asked the Native Americans how they felt about this.)

In 1806, mountain man **Zebulon Pike** led a group of American explorers into Colorado, but he and his men were captured by the Spanish and sent back to the United States. The argument over who owned Colorado went on until the signing of the **Adams-Onis Treaty**

"The Emigrants" by Frederic Remington

"Westward the Course of Empire Takes Its Way" by Emanuel Leutze

in 1819. Through this treaty, the United States purchased Florida, but agreed to give up all claims to Colorado. The Spanish government was happy. It looked like it would hold onto Colorado forever.

However, in 1821 Mexico won its independence from Spain through the Mexican War of Independence. Colorado then became part of Mexico. After less than two years, Spain had lost Colorado again!

As settlers to New Mexico (which you will read about soon) began to move through this hot, dry area, there was a need for supplies and water. In 1833, a **trading post**, or place where Native Americans and settlers could buy and trade goods and supplies, was founded. This was Bent's Fort, Colorado's first

non-native settlement. This trading post soon became an important stop on the **Santa Fe Trail**—a dangerous, 900-mile trail from Franklin, Missouri to Santa Fe, New Mexico.

The Santa Fe Trail passed through perilous deserts and mountains. Travelers were at constant risk from bandits, Native Americans, and rattlesnakes. Before railroads, travelers had no choice but to use the Santa Fe Trail, so the watering holes of Bent's Fort were always a welcome sight. So many Americans followed this trail into Mexican territory that it eventually became one cause of the **Mexican-American War**. When Mexico lost the war in 1848, it gave up much of the northern part of its territory, including Colorado, to the United States.

Despite the constant struggle by many governments to control Colorado, in the end very few settlers actually wanted to live there. For the most part, gold-seekers on their way to Oregon and California tried to pass through the Rocky Mountains as quickly as possible.

However, in 1859, several groups of people heading to California decided to try their luck panning for gold in Colorado's South Platte River. Rumors of the small nuggets they found launched the **Pike's Peak Gold Rush**. Over 100,000 "fifty-niners" rushed into the mountains of Colorado to seek their fortunes. Very few people got rich, but settlers kept coming. Sadly, conflict with Native American tribes led to the **Colorado War**. Afterwards, most of the Arapaho, Cheyenne, Comanche, Shoshone, and Ute people were forced onto reservations. In 1876—one hundred years after the signing of the Declaration of Independence—Colorado joined the Union as "the Centennial State."

The Rocky Mountains cross through more than half of Colorado, easily making it our highest and most mountainous state. The majestic view from the top of Pike's Peak inspired Katherine Lee Bates to write "America the Beautiful."

In between the mountains are high valleys called "parks." One park is larger than the entire state of Connecticut! However, most people live east of the mountains, in the flatter part of the state at the edge of the Great Plains; here you will find the "Mile-High City" of Denver.

The Colorado River is the longest river west of the Rocky Mountains. Dams on the Arkansas, Rio Grande, and South Platte bring much-needed water to Colorado farms, where cattle and sheep are raised and wheat and corn are grown. Gold and silver are still mined, but coal, iron, oil, and natural gas are now the most important natural resources.

Mountain resorts like Aspen, Colorado, attract millions of skiers each year. At Mesa Verde you can see mysterious and ancient Native American cliff dwellings built right into the sides of stone cliffs. At nearby Four Corners, do the impossible: stand in four states all at the same time!

Student Workbook: Complete pg. 69.

"Pike's Peak" by Albert Bierstadt

Colorado's
Catholic Heritage

The Story of Sr. Blandina Segale

Cowboys, rustlers, bandits, outlaws, and...nuns? Books and movies are filled with tall tales of Wild West gunfights, but less known are the stories of nuns who tried to bring civilization into what was sometimes a very uncivilized place. The story of **Sister Blandina Segale** could be the tallest tale of all—but it's absolutely true!

As a little girl in Cincinnati, Ohio, Blandina often begged the nuns at her school to retell stories about how they once brought comfort to wounded soldiers on Civil War battlefields—bullets whizzed by and cannonballs exploded, while the nuns were armed with only their Faith. These stories filled Blandina's young mind. She prayed each night to become a nun—and to find her own adventure in the West. It all seemed so exciting!

In 1872, Sr. Blandina took her final vows as a nun and received word that her request to head West had been granted. She hurriedly told her father the exciting news but, to her sadness,

he begged her to stay. Her father had always supported her in everything else before, so Sr. Blandina was surprised. Her father explained that stories and real life can be quite different—that the West is filled with bad men and other dangers—but he knew she had made up her mind.

As soon as the train pulled out of the station, Sr. Blandina began to tell the other passengers about her mission. Most repeated her father's words. They warned her that cowboys could not be trusted; she should go home immediately!

By the time Sr. Blandina reached the end of the railroad line, she felt very uncertain. She now had to make a choice: take the train back home to civilization, or catch a ride on a stagecoach into the dangerous unknown. She clutched her rosary tightly. The stagecoach it was!

After a frightening trip she finally reached her destination—Trinidad, Colorado. Lying near the end of the Santa Fe Trail, Trinidad had a reputa-

Sr. Blandina's students

tion as a place where criminals hid out in between murders and robberies. No one here wanted to listen to God—much less to a nun! One day, while Sister was trying to teach children about forgiveness, an angry mob hanged a man outside the classroom window.

Another time, two gunslingers who were gang members of Billy the Kid rode into Trinidad. For days they terrorized the town, until the two men began to argue between themselves: both drew their guns and fired! One man died, while the other (named Schneider) was severely wounded in his leg. The townspeople, taking their revenge, threw the wounded man into an abandoned mine outside of town.

While the townspeople celebrated, Sr. Blandina entered the dark mine alone with food and blankets. She nursed the dying outlaw back to health, visiting him every day for four months. At first, Schneider bragged of his misdeeds. He said he was proud to be going to hell! In response, Sr. Blandina brought him a burning coal on a shovel. She said if he was that unafraid of hell he wouldn't mind touching the coal as a preview! Schneider was impressed by

Sr. Blandina's "guts"—she was as tough as any cowboy. All the while she reminded him that God can forgive any sin—no matter how great.

One day, Schneider warned Sr. Blandina that the outlaw Billy the Kid was coming to town to get revenge on the townspeople for leaving Schneider to die. Sr. Blandina raced back to town, not certain what to do. When the people of Trinidad caught sight of the outlaw riding angrily into their town, everyone ran and hid. Everyone except Sr. Blandina.

Billy knew she must be the one who saved Schneider's life. He took her hand and promised to grant her any favor, no matter how great. She asked him simply to leave the town in peace. Although an outlaw, Billy was a man of his word. When the frightened townspeople emerged from their hiding-places, Billy was gone.

Because of a servant of Christ, an evil man had shown mercy. But how much greater is God's mercy! Sister Blandina had saved the lives of the townspeople. Now they were finally ready for her to help them save their souls.

New Mexico

Lured by tales of the "Seven Golden Cities of Cibola," Spanish explorer **Francisco Coronado** ventured into the hostile desert north of Mexico in 1540. (New Mexico seemed an appropriate name.) After a perilous journey, he was outraged to discover that the "Golden Cities" were just a series of seven humble villages made of adobe (a mixture of sand and mud).

Perhaps to get the angry stranger to leave, a Zuni tribesman told Coronado of a city of gold farther away. Coronado rushed on to continue his search, but never found the riches he was searching for. What a shame. In his blind chase after wealth, Coronado missed the real treasure he had discovered.

Cliff dwellings

The apartment-like **cliff dwellings** (sometimes called "pueblos") built into the sides of cliffs by many southwestern Native American tribes are wondrous to behold. Native peoples have lived in them for hundreds of years and some still live in them today. These pueblos are scattered throughout one of the most awe-inspiring landscapes in the world. Coronado couldn't see this beauty, even though it was all around him. Don't make the same mistake in your own life!

"Coronado Sets Out to the North" by Frederic Remington

163

Even though Coronado left disappointed, many Spanish ranchers and missionaries followed over the next several years. In 1608, La Villa Real de la Santa Fé de San Francisco de Asís (The Royal Town of the Holy Faith of Saint Francis of Assisi) was founded. We now call the city simply Santa Fe—the oldest capital city in the United States. New Mexico's modern government still meets in the Palace of the Governors, built many centuries ago.

While most of New Mexico remained under Spanish control for generations, the northeastern tip was claimed by France and was sold to the United States in the Louisiana Purchase.

Built in 1610, this Santa Fe, New Mexico church is the oldest church building in the U.S.

When Mexico became independent from Spain through the Mexican War of Independence, New Mexico became a part of "Old" Mexico. However, a large part was claimed by the short-lived Republic of Texas in 1836.

The Santa Fe Trail brought more than 5,000 American wagon trains a year into New Mexico. (You remember that the increasing number of American immigrants into Mexican territory was one of the leading causes of the Mexican-American War.) After the U.S. won the Mexican-American War, New Mexico became a U.S. possession under the terms of the **Treaty of Guadalupe Hidalgo** in 1848.

In the Compromise of 1850, Texas also gave up its claims to New Mexico for $10 million. Finally, a small portion of southwestern New Mexico still under Mexican control (called the Bootheel) was bought by the United States in the **Gadsden Purchase** of 1853.

Although not yet a state at the time of the Civil War (1861-1865), critical battles were fought in New Mexico in a struggle to control the southwest. At this same time, thousands of Navajos and other Native Americans were force-marched into reservations. Then, after the Civil War, railroads slowly brought in even more settlers, and in 1912 New Mexico became the 47th state.

New Mexico is the fifth largest state, and is known for its mountains, **mesas** (high, flat-topped areas of land), and

New Mexico has a higher percentage of Native Americans and Hispanics than any other state in the **contiguous** (connected 48 states) United States. Spanish missions, pow-wows, and fiestas attract many tourists, while artists find inspiration from the natural wonders of "The Land of Enchantment."

magnificent deserts. Although New Mexico's climate is mostly dry and sunny, the snow-capped peaks of the Rocky Mountains stretch from the north down to the center of the state. In the northwest is the Colorado Plateau—an area of mesas and forest wilderness. Beautiful rock formations like Ship Rock can be found here. The eastern third of New Mexico lies in the Great Plains, while deserts stretch across the southern part of the state. The Rio Grande River flows south through the middle of the state, bringing much needed water.

Most of New Mexico's jobs come from drilling and mining oil, natural gas, potash, copper, silver, and uranium. New Mexico farmers grow more chili peppers than in any other state, and some cattle ranches in New Mexico cover more than 100 square miles! The first atomic bomb was tested in the New Mexico desert—nuclear and space research is still performed here.

Atomic bomb test in Los Alamos, New Mexico

Priscilla, June 24, 1957

165

Cliff dwellings

Imagine that you are trotting on horseback through desert **canyons** in the Southwest. Towering, rocky cliffs rise high into the sky on your left and on your right. As your horse comes around a hilly bend, you gasp—ahead lies a silent, empty city, carved into the mountainside cliffs. Who once lived here? Where did the people go?

Let's find out!

Long, long ago, native peoples built towns and cities like the Gila Cliff Dwellings, those at Chaco Canyon, Puye Cliffs, and Taos Pueblo in New Mexico. (Arizona's Tonto Basin and Colorado's Mesa Verde have similar "silent cities.")

Some of these towns and cities were carved right into the cliffs, and stretched for almost a mile along the mountainside! Many of the houses or rooms could be reached only by very tall ladders. If there was danger of attack, the people who lived inside could simply pull the ladder up and no one could climb in.

Other pueblos were built with blocks cut from stone. The stones were placed together to construct thick-walled buildings, two, three, and four stories tall!

Some of these dwellings were built more than a thousand years ago, but they still stand as a reminder of the proud people who once lived there.

Where did the people go? The descendents of the Hopi, Pueblo, Apache, and Navajo still live in the Southwest. But most of their ancient cities were abandoned, for different reasons. But you can find out why. Now that you have some clues, put on your detective hat and see what you can discover!

New Mexico's
Catholic Heritage

The Story of Las Posadas

According to legend, in 1325 a small group of wandering Native Americans saw a vision of an eagle perched on a cactus, eating a snake. They interpreted this vision to mean their wandering days were over. There they built a city called Tenochtitlan and from that legendary beginning grew one of the world's greatest and most impressive civilizations—the Aztecs.

Within 200 years of their founding, the **Aztecs** had formed the largest empire in North American history, battling and destroying other tribes in what we now call Mexico. The Aztecs believed their success came from pleasing the many gods they worshiped. They believed that Huitzilopochtli—their sun-god of war—demanded constant human sacrifice. Members of tribes conquered by the Aztecs were often sacrificed in these bloody rituals.

When Spanish missionaries first arrived in Mexico in the 16th century, they were shocked by the horrific Aztec practice of human sacrifice. However,

Aztecs cruelly sacrificed thousands of neighboring tribesmen to false gods.

some missionaries saw that the Aztec culture had much good in it, too. (Don't let anyone ever tell you any group of people is "all good" or "all bad.") Sadly, the missionaries found the enthusiasm that the Aztecs had for their false religion was often greater than European Christians had for their true religion. (Happily, most of the Aztecs enthusiastically embraced Christianity after Our Lady of Guadalupe appeared to St. Juan Diego, but that is another story.)

Our Lady of Guadalupe,
patroness of the Americas,
pray for us!

One ancient Aztec celebration honored the legendary birth of the false god Huitzilopochtli. In celebration, Aztecs traveled from house to house singing. Once inside, a great party was held

with food and dancing. By coincidence, this festival was held at the same time as Christmas. The missionaries did not demand that the Aztecs throw away the good with the bad. Why not continue this festival, but instead of using it to honor the birth of a false and bloodthirsty god, use it to honor the birth of the true and loving God? A unique tradition called Las Posadas was born.

The Aztec empire was eventually destroyed by the Spanish military (not everyone can see the good from the bad), but Las Posadas lives on. The tradition soon spread to other Spanish-speaking parts of North America. Today, it has become an important part of Hispanic-American Catholic culture, especially in New Mexico.

Almost every parish with a Hispanic population in New Mexico performs their own version of Las Posadas. The details are a little different in every parish, but the story of Las Posadas is the same everywhere: the congregation walks from house to house, re-enacting Mary and Joseph's journey to Bethlehem in search of an inn. (Las Posadas is Spanish for "the inns.")

The journey usually takes the form of a novena, spread out over the nine nights before Christmas. Each night the congregation meets for Mass at the Church before walking to the house of a parishioner that serves as the "inn" that night. Usually, Mary and Joseph are played by young children riding a real donkey! Other children dress as angels (to remind us of heaven) and others as shepherds (to remind us of our earthly life.) Someone inside the house plays the innkeeper. (Sometimes a man dressed as the devil plays the innkeeper, jumping around and trying to scare everyone!) The group of *peregrinos* (travelers) outside sings a song asking to be let in, while the group inside sings a song telling them to go away.

After three verses, the inside group finally invites the *peregrinos* in. Once inside the house, everyone prays a part of the novena, inviting the Holy Family into their hearts as well as their home. After the prayer the host family presents a huge feast of traditional Hispanic foods like tamales, empanadas, and bizchochitos—the New Mexico state cookie! Finally, a star-shaped piñata is broken. Candy pours out, symbolizing the sweetness of "breaking" through our sins.

Las Posadas is just one example of how every culture adds something special to the Catholic Church—the Universal Church—in America and the world. What a boring world it would be if we were all the same. Our differences are worth sharing and celebrating!

Star-shaped Las Posadas piñata

A Las Posadas procession

Arizona

Phoenix

The Spanish ruled Arizona from the 1500s until the Mexican Revolution in 1821. After the Mexican-American War, Arizona was given to the United States and in 1912 it became the 48th state—the final state of the contiguous states. Native American warriors like **Geronimo** fought against white settlement, and Arizona still has one of the largest Native American populations in the country. Almost 25% of Arizona's population is Hispanic; Cesar Chavez, who worked for Hispanic-American civil rights, was born in Arizona.

Most of Arizona is blistering hot desert, but the weather is ideal for growing cotton, lettuce, and cantaloupe. Mining is the most important industry—two-thirds of the nation's copper comes from Arizona mines. Most manufacturing is done in Phoenix, the capital and our country's sixth-largest city.

Have you ever heard of the Gunfight at the O.K. Corral? It happened in the city of Tombstone, and is surely the most famous Old West shootout of all time.

Arizona has more national monuments than any other state. The Painted Desert (the layers of colorful rocks do look like someone painted them), the Petrified Forest (the trees have turned to stone!), and Meteor Crater (where a 60,000 ton meteorite once struck the earth) are just a few of Arizona's natural wonders. However, "The Grand Canyon State" is best known for its mile-deep, 18-mile-wide, and 277-mile-long canyon.

Grand Canyon

Idaho

With the Louisiana Purchase of 1803, the size of the United States almost doubled. What was this enormous new territory like? Were there new animals and plants to be found there? Might there even be a river or some waterway that could be used for travel, and maybe even open a new route to Asia? No one knew. So President Jefferson sent explorers Meriwether Lewis and William Clark on a journey of discovery to find out; this journey, which you read about when we studied Missouri and North Dakota, became known as the **Lewis and Clark Expedition**. (Look at a map to see how far Idaho and Louisiana are from each other!)

Some of the territory that Lewis and Clark explored would later become Idaho. Even before Lewis and Clark arrived, French-Canadian and Catholic Iroquois trappers could be found in Idaho. Through their influence, Fr. Pierre de Smet was summoned by the region's native peoples in the 1840s. The first permanent settlement in Idaho was founded by Mormon settlers in 1860, but a brief gold rush brought Irish Catholics into the area. They, too, brought Catholic influence to the area. Of course, many other fortune seekers raced to Idaho, swelling the population so that statehood was achieved in 1890.

Father de Smet traveling in the Rockies, by Bill Gollings

Although most of the gold is now gone, mining is still very important to the Gem State—almost every type of gemstone in the world can be found somewhere in Idaho. Also, more silver is mined in Idaho than in any other state. Most of the state is mountainous and much of it is covered by lush forests—lumber is a major industry. Idaho's manufacturing jobs mostly involve food processing and chemicals, while farms grow barley, sugar beets, and wheat. However, Idaho's best known crop is its potatoes—more are grown in the Potato State than in any other.

Although Idaho is larger than all the New England states put together, it has one of the smallest populations of any state. Most people live fewer than 30 miles from the Snake River in the southern part of the state, where you can find Hell's Canyon—the deepest canyon in North America.

Dams on Idaho's rivers produce most of Idaho's electricity. If you like adventures on the water, these same rivers also create the conditions for thrilling white-water rafting.

Old Ignace and Fr. Pierre De Smet

Old Ignace was both an Iroquois Catholic and a Canadian fur trader. The fur-trading expeditions of Old Ignace eventually led him and 23 other Iroquois to settle in Montana with the Flathead (Salish) tribe. In their new home, they taught the eager Flatheads about Our Lord and His Church. Not only the Flatheads, but also members of neighboring tribes such as the Nez Perce in present-day Idaho, became faithful Catholics, evangelized by other Native American Catholics!

These Flatheads, Nez Perce, and Iroquois now began to yearn for a priest to teach them more about Our Lord and to bring them the Sacraments. Unfortunately, as far as the Flatheads knew, the nearest priests were in St. Louis, Missouri—more than 1,500 miles away! It was decided that volunteers from the tribes would be sent to St. Louis to try to bring back a priest, but many of these volunteers died on the way, including Old Ignace himself. Finally, Young Ignace, Old Ignace's son, bravely set out to try once more. In St. Louis, the missionary Belgian priest, Fr. Pierre De Smet, was touched by their earnest request for "Black Robes," and he decided to offer himself in their service.

In March of 1840, Fr. De Smet and Young Ignace began their long and difficult journey back to Montana. Besides enduring thirst, exhaustion, and fear of hostile tribes, Fr. De Smet suffered from bouts of malaria. When he was too ill to stay in the saddle, Fr. De Smet travelled in the back of the supply wagon, which bounced and jolted over the rough, roadless terrain.

After several months, Young Ignace and the "Black Robe" arrived at the home of the Flatheads. Within the first two months, Fr. De Smet had baptized 600 men, women, and children, including the chiefs of the Flatheads. All this was due to the courage of Fr. De Smet and the perseverance of Old Ignace and his Catholic family and friends, who were willing to sacrifice even their lives to bring the Faith to their people.

Montana

"Montana" is Spanish for mountain—seventy-seven different ranges of the Rocky Mountains pass through the western part of this state. The rest of the state is "Big Sky Country"—the open prairies of the Great Plains. Even in this flatter area a number of "island ranges" rise up, so Montana truly earns its name. These two areas are split by the **Continental Divide** high in the mountains—waters that begin with rain and snowfall in the mountains on the western side of the Divide eventually drain into the Pacific Ocean; waters on the eastern side drain into the distant Atlantic Ocean.

The United States bought most of Montana from France through the Louisiana Purchase. When William Clark scratched a few words into **Pompey's Pillar** he left the only physical evidence that the famed Lewis and Clark expedition had passed through. (Pompey's Pillar is a tall, rocky "hill" climbed by William Clark.) During their exploration, the explorers discovered the source of the Missouri River in Montana.

Fur trading and the discovery of gold and silver in the mid-1800s encouraged many settlers to come to this state. Their arrival led to fierce fighting with Native American tribes. **Little Big Horn** was the site of "Custer's Last Stand" in 1876, in which warriors led by Lakota Chiefs **Sitting Bull** and **Crazy Horse** defeated **General George Armstrong Custer** and his troops. (You can visit the site of this famous battle at the Custer Battlefield National Monument in southeastern Montana.) Many Native Americans still live in Montana, and cowboy culture continues to thrive—almost every town has a rodeo.

Montana farmers grow barley, wheat, and sugar beets. Oil reserves add to the economy.

"Custer's Last Stand" by Harold Von Schmidt

173

Nevada

© Carson City

Spain was the first to claim Nevada, which eventually became a part of independent Mexico. The United States took control following the Mexican-American War in 1848. The first settlers were groups of Mormons who arrived throughout the 1850s. In 1859 the **Comstock Lode** was discovered—the richest deposit of silver ever found in the United States. With this discovery, people who hoped to make a fortune in the silver mines rushed into the territory. Almost overnight, a booming town—a "boom town"—developed around the mines at Virginia City. (Many of the original buildings, including a Catholic parish and hospital, still stand and are open to visitors.) Even today, Nevada leads all states in gold and silver mining, as well as the mining of turquoise.

Turquoise jewelry

During the Civil War, the **13th Amendment to the Constitution**, which would make slavery illegal, was proposed in Congress. If this Amendment passed, slavery in the United States would finally be outlawed forever. Unfortunately, the Amendment needed three more votes to pass. What could be done?

President Lincoln suggested that Nevada be admitted as a new state. In 1864, "The Battle Born State" joined the Union and immediately cast its three votes for the 13th Amendment. The evil of slavery was over!

The gambling industry provides for one-third of Nevada's jobs, especially under the neon lights of Las Vegas.

Nevada is the driest state in the country, but the Hoover Dam (the world's largest) brings water and electric power to a thirsty and growing population. Farms grow garlic, alfalfa and mint. The mountains and barren deserts of Nevada have always made it difficult for people to live here, but bristle-cone pines thrive in this climate—these pines are the world's oldest living things!

Aerial view of the Hoover Dam

Utah

For thousands of years, the Ute tribe inhabited the land that now takes their name. The Spanish arrived in the 1500s, but showed little interest in settling this region of mountains and deserts. Utah became a part of independent Mexico before passing to the United States after the Mexican-American War in 1848. Statehood was granted in 1896.

Franciscan missionaries are known to have instructed natives in the area as early as 1776, and it was the great Catholic missionary to the western tribes, Fr. Pierre de Smet, who told Mormon leader Brigham Young and

his followers about the Great Salt Lake and the surrounding valley! (Do you remember reading about Fr. de Smet's earlier travels to Idaho?) Young led his followers from faraway Illinois to Utah's Great Salt Lake in 1847. Today, more than 60% of Utahans belong to the Mormon religion, which still heavily influences the culture of the state.

One very important event that linked the long-settled eastern United States with the Wild West happened right here in Utah. Both ends of the *Transcontinental Railroad* finally met at *Promontory Point*, Utah, in 1869—for the first

Celebrating the completion of the first transcontinental railroad of the USA at Promontory Summit, Utah: "The Ceremony of the Golden Spike on May 10, 1869" by Dean Cornwall

time, the entire United States, from the Atlantic to the Pacific, was connected by railroad! This meant that people and goods no longer had to travel for months in slow-moving wagons along dangerous trails to reach their destinations. Before, people often lost their possessions and lives in the deserts and mountains of the West, but now they could travel far more quickly, and safely, by train.

Like so many other western states, Utah contains part of the Rocky Mountains. The Rocky Mountains cut through northern and central Utah, and the Colorado Plateau is in southern Utah. The mostly barren and dry Great Basin is in western Utah, where you can go swimming in the Great Salt Lake. Try as you might, you can't sink because of the lake's high salt content!

Utahans find employment drilling for oil and natural gas, and mining coal, copper, and iron. Utah's factories then refine these natural resources. Other Utahans raise cattle and sheep on this state's range lands.

Surely you have seen one of the "image dissector tubes" of Philo T. Farnsworth, a Utah scientist and inventor? You probably call it a television!

Philo Farnsworth with an early TV

176

Cheyenne ⊙

Wyoming

In the nineteenth century, thousands passed through Wyoming on their way to settle in California and Oregon, but the difficult **terrain**, or land, of jagged mountains and deep canyons discouraged settlers from staying long.

When the Transcontinental Railroad was built, it made the trip through Wyoming easier, but towns also started growing up along the railroad's route. In 1890, "The Equality State" joined the Union. The state got its nickname because women had been granted the right to vote in Wyoming in 1869, fifty years before the federal government guaranteed that right across the country. Wyoming's Nellie Tayloe Ross was the first female governor of any state, and Esther Hobart Morris was the nation's first female judge.

Wyoming is the tenth largest state, but it has fewer people than any other state. Mining is the most important industry; oil, natural gas, uranium, and coal are found here. (The nation's ten largest coal mines are in Wyoming.)

Most of the state lies within the Rocky Mountains, but the eastern third is in the Great Plains, which is perfect for cattle and sheep ranching.

"Old Faithful"

When early Wyoming explorers and mountain men told stories of trees made of stone, rivers of steam, and bubbling streams of mud, people found them so unbelievable that they thought the stories were myths. But you can see for yourself that they are true—at Yellowstone, the world's first national park and the home of "Old Faithful," the world's most famous geyser. Every 91 minutes it erupts. Every time! Honest!

Student Workbook: Complete pgs. 70-71.

Preparing to Learn about My State

You will soon begin learning about the Pacific states, the last region in our study of these great United States. But let's take a moment's peek at what's coming soon after!

Long before your parents or grandparents or great grandparents were born, Native Americans lived in your state. What do you know about these ancient peoples?

You can find out about them by visiting places where these first residents lived. If you live in New Mexico, for example, you can visit the Gila and Puye Cliff Dwellings, where these ancient peoples lived long ago. How were their lives different from yours? How were they the same?

After a time, explorers, missionaries, and settlers came from Europe to explore, to spread the good news about Jesus, and to build a new life in your state. Who lived in your state long ago, hundreds of years before your parents or grandparents or great grandparents were born? How can you find out?

A good place to begin the search for answers is in your state capitol, sometimes called a statehouse. The state capitol is the place where your state government is located. People who have been elected to lead your state, such as your governor, senators, and representatives, work here.

But state capitols also have information about the beginnings, or history, of your state. Often, capitol walls are covered with murals, or paintings, that tell the history of the state. Capitol guides give tours that teach about state history and government.

Capitol buildings also have museum stores or gift shops that are filled with books, DVDs, and other materials that tell the amazing story of your state. There are books for adults, and books for children; books about places to visit; and exciting stories of early peoples and settlers.

The very best way that you can begin your state study is with a visit to your state capitol. During your visit, you will begin to have your questions answered, and you can select and bring home materials that will make your state study exciting. Plan to begin your state study with such a visit, *at least a week or two before you begin the State Study unit in your workbook.*

If it simply isn't possible to visit your statehouse, virtual tours are available online. These tours are usually linked to your state capitol's website; by browsing

the website you may also find and order materials about your state.

Virtual tours may be found at the following internet sites, or by typing "virtual tour + [name of your state] + capitol building" in a search engine.

http://jfredpeterson.com/lindsey/statecap.htm

When you studied social studies or history in the past, you may have used textbooks for most of your study. As you mature, or grow up in body, mind, and soul, you will begin to take more and more responsibility for finding information about topics outside of textbooks. This doesn't mean that textbooks are not valuable, or that you will no longer use them. Textbooks are a good starting point in learning.

But to really understand a subject, we often need to research, or search for materials about a subject, beyond the textbook. Your state study is a good time to learn research skills that you will use in later grades.

There are many places to find more information, including books from the library or bookstore; on the internet; watching DVDs; and visiting places where you can learn more about your subject.

If you haven't already done so, please begin now to gather the materials that you will use to research about your state. (Your parents will need to know about this, too, so please ask them to read these two pages.)

For this state study, you will need a 3-ring binder with a clear plastic cover and an inside pocket to hold papers that are not 3-hole-punched. This binder will store your state study projects and activities; it will become a permanent record of your state study.

And now, back to discover more about these great United States!

Resources

- As always, a set of encyclopedias is a valuable resource for information about individual states, including maps, state history, climate, industry, and much more.
- Your local library will have a good selection of books, encyclopedias, and videos or DVDs with information about your state.
- Your state capitol museum/gift shop will have a good selection of books and videos or DVDs as well.
- Auto travel clubs offer free state tour books to members; these books contain locations of museums and historical sites that you can visit.
- The internet offers a great number of sites that link to information about your state, from free outline maps to video clips of important events in your state history.

  http://awesomeamerica.com/
  http://www.ipl.org/div/stateknow/
  http://www.50states.com/
  http://www.e-referencedesk.com/resources/state/
  (sidebar on left of page includes information on state's history, geography, economy, and more)
  http://www.infoplease.com/states.html
  http://www.history.com/topics/states

Search engine ideas:
   your state name + historical society
   your state name + history online
   your state name + historical museum
   your state name + economy
   your state name + natural resources
   your state name + historical sites
   your state name + historical landmarks

Alaska

California

Hawaii

Oregon

Washington

Pacific
REGION

The Pacific states of the Western United States are: **Alaska, California, Hawaii, Oregon**, and **Washington**.

The Pacific States lie along (or in) the world's largest ocean. Mountains lie along the Pacific Coast, and lead into the fertile valleys where much of the country's food is grown. In the north, lush forests thrive—logging has always been an important industry here.

To the south, along California's coastline, you'll find a string of historic Catholic missions started by Father Junipero Serra in the mid-1700s; Spanish settlers slowly followed. As in the case of many other western states, the United States gained California after the Mexican-American War. A year later, in 1849, the California Gold Rush would attract many more settlers.

At the same time, confusion with England over the ownership of Oregon and Washington led to a peaceful treaty granting that land to the United States. The Oregon and California Trails brought many settlers into these new lands, but you remember that it was the completion of the Transcontinental Railroad that finally connected the eastern and western halves of our country.

Rounding out our Pacific states are Alaska and Hawaii, the only non-contiguous states—that is, those not connected to any of the other 48 states. (Alaska was purchased from Russia in 1867, and Hawaii became a possession of the United States in 1898.)

Along the northern Pacific coast, summers are cool and dry, while winters are rainy. The southern coast enjoys warm, dry summers and winters! (Would you like to grow bananas? You can, if you live in southern California!)

Alaska and Hawaii have unique but opposite climates: Alaska has bitterly cold, unbelievably snowy winters and cool summers, while tropical Hawaii is warm and sunny most of the year.

Turn to **LESSONS ALIVE!** on pgs. 72-73 of your workbook for enrichment activities.

Alaska

America has always been a nation of immigrants—even longer ago than we once imagined. In fact, more than 12,000 years ago, during the last Ice Age, giant glaciers created a blockage that lowered the ocean levels in Alaska's Bering Strait. This created a "land bridge" in the middle of the ocean! Ancient Asian peoples walked across this land bridge from Siberia (in modern-day Russia) and found themselves in what we now call Alaska.

When the glaciers melted, the ocean level rose and the land bridge was swallowed up. The descendants of those early immigrants were cut off forever from their ancient homes, but they began slowly to spread throughout North and South America. Over time, hundreds of Native American tribes—descendants of these first immigrants to Alaska—would fill this new land. Cut off from the rest of the world, it would be thousands of years before the **Aleut**, the **Inuit** (or Eskimos), and all the other Native American tribes would encounter more immigrants, also coming from across the ocean.

In the 1700s the Russians became the first Europeans to reach Alaska, founding several small fur-trading settlements, some as far south as the coast of California! However, by 1867 the Russian economy was in trouble and **Czar Alexander II** (the king of Russia) was looking for ways to refill his empty treasury.

U.S. Secretary of State **William H. Seward** made a deal with Russia to buy Alaska for $7.2 million. That might sound like a lot, but Alaska is so big that the price broke down to less than two cents an acre! Despite the cheap price tag, many Americans thought it was still a waste of money. Perceived by many Americans as an empty and frozen wasteland, Alaska became

An Aleut seal-hunter in the Bering Sea, 1816, by Louis Choris

Mount McKinley

mockingly known as "Seward's Icebox" and "Seward's Folly." (A folly is a stupid mistake.)

In 1880, Joe Juneau discovered gold in southern Alaska; sixteen years later, even more gold discoveries were made in Alaska's Yukon. Thousands of people joined the **Alaska Gold Rush**. Very few got rich, but many made homes for themselves in this beautiful land. Jack London's adventures in Alaska inspired him to write some of America's best-loved books, like *Call of the Wild* and *White Fang.*

Nowadays, it isn't gold but "black gold" that fuels the state's economy. Since the discovery of huge oil reserves in 1968, oil production has become Alaska's primary industry. About 88,000 barrels of crude oil move through the Alaska Pipeline every hour! In this vast wilderness, petroleum companies follow strict rules that allow oil supplies to the rest of the states to keep flowing, but also keep Alaskan plants and animals thriving.

No one's laughing at "Seward's Folly" now!

Since Alaska's climate is so cold, very little farming is done here, but the ocean and rivers provide an abundance of fish, which is shipped all over the world. The timber industry is also a big part of Alaska's economy.

Off the coast of Alaska, the Aleutian Islands—a series of more than 300 volcanic islands—stretch into the Pacific Ocean for 1,200 miles. During World War II, the Japanese invaded these islands. So that the U.S. military could transport troops and equipment to defend this territory, it built the 1,422-mile Alaska Highway in less than eight months! Although originally built for this military purpose, the highway—which stretches through Canada all the way to Alaska—opened Alaska up to further settlement. In 1959, Alaska joined the Union as our 49th state. History had come full circle. In a way, weren't the very first Americans from Alaska?

The Aleutian word Alaxsxaq (Alaska) means "shore" and with 34,000 miles of shoreline, the name fits. Alaska is completely surrounded by water, except in the east where it borders Canada. Alaska is at least 500 miles away from every other state, but it is by far the largest state—making up one-sixth of our country's total area. Only 18 *countries* are bigger!

The northernmost third of Alaska lies within the Arctic Circle. Barrow, America's northernmost city, is less than 1,200 miles from the North Pole! Because Barrow is so far north, in the summer the people here get 84 continuous days when the sun never sets. In the winter, they get 69 days of complete darkness!

This enormous state, if picked up by a giant helicopter and dropped across the rest of the United States, would cover most of Kansas, Missouri, Illinois, Iowa, Wisconsin, Minnesota, and more! Yet, only 1% of this huge state is owned by private individuals. The rest of the land is owned by the federal government (65%), by the state, and by Native American tribes.

Most of Alaska is a sparsely inhabited, but breathtaking, frozen tundra. Most people live along the southern coast where the weather is mildest. In modern towns along the coastline, elements of frontier life can still be found. No roads lead to the outside world, so Juneau, the state capital, can be reached only by boat or plane.

Aurora borealis

Sled dog race

In Alaska you can find Mount McKinley, America's highest peak. Bears, caribou, and moose run free.

Yell "Mush!" at the Iditarod Sled Dog Race and marvel at the ***aurora borealis***—brilliantly colored streamers of light that sometimes fill Alaska's night sky.

Student Workbook: Complete pgs. 74-75.

183

Alaska's

Catholic Heritage

The Story of Bishop Seghers

No Catholic priest had ever set foot in cold and distant Alaska before it was purchased by the United States. It would take a special kind of man to want to venture into that harsh wilderness! One day, that special man arrived—**Bishop Charles John Seghers**.

Born in Belgium, the young Seghers dreamed of being a missionary in North America. After his ordination to the priesthood in 1863, he was sent to Vancouver Island in Canada. Father Seghers threw himself into his missionary work to both native people and pioneers. He taught in two Catholic schools and even put together the first choir in the Cathedral.

Bishop Demers, the Bishop of Vancouver Island, started calling Father Seghers "half of myself." For ten years Bishop Demers and Father Seghers worked side by side on North America's largest island. Even though Father Seghers was only 33 years old when Bishop Demers died, he was the natural choice to become the new bishop. In 1873, Bishop Seghers took his place as North America's youngest bishop.

Less than three weeks after his ordination, the new bishop surprised everyone by packing his bags and announcing he was taking a journey. He was going to visit the lone priest ministering at the only missionary station in far-off Alaska. Technically, this vast land was a part of his diocese, and if he was to be its bishop, how could he ignore it? Alaska was a land filled with native people who had never heard the Good News of the Catholic Church, not through their own fault, but because no Catholic had dared to bring it to them. Bishop Seghers vowed to change that.

Although Bishop Seghers' first visit to Alaska was a brief one, it was enough time for him to realize how much he was needed. In spite of the harsh, bitterly cold environment, Bishop Seghers' heart warmed to the needs of the native villagers he encountered.

He returned to his home on Vancouver Island (where he established several new missions, and built the first Catholic school and hospital), all the while planning a return trip to the Alaskan wilderness.

In 1877, Bishop Seghers traveled once again into that distant land, founding missions all along the Yukon River and preaching in native villages. He earned the respect of friendly native people by learning their language and enduring the unfriendly environment with a smile seldom seen on outsiders' faces. Bishop Seghers traveled 2,500 miles in 14 months before returning home, where he received some shocking news—he was to be transferred to Oregon.

Bishop Seghers accepted his new assignment and accomplished great things there too, but his heart longed to return to his Alaska missions. There was still so much work to be done. To make matters worse, the Church could find no one suitable to replace Bishop Seghers in Vancouver Island and Alaska. Everyone thought the job was too hard. When he heard this, Bishop Seghers begged Pope Leo XIII to return him to his old diocese. The Pope consented and, by 1885, Bishop Seghers was back on Vancouver Island. Within a few months of arriving, Bishop Seghers' bags were packed again. Everyone knew what that meant. He was off to Alaska!

The following year, Bishop Seghers made his final trip into Alaska. He was willing to die where few were willing to live. Other brave men and women have followed his example, but there is still a lot more work to be done. Today, the Diocese of Fairbanks, Alaska is our nation's largest diocese, but there is only one priest for every 20,000 square miles! The days of the missionaries are not over. There are people in parts of the world—in your own country, in your own neighborhood—who may never know Christ if we aren't willing to bring Him to them. Will *you?*

Sacred Heart Cathedral in Fairbanks, Alaska, the northern-most cathedral in the world

California

Sacramento

A popular Spanish novel in the 1500s told of wild adventures on the imaginary island of California. In the book, California is a beautiful paradise filled with gold, gold, and more gold! After Spanish sailors Diego de Becerra and Fortun Ximenez discovered what they thought was an island off the west coast of North America in 1533, mapmakers named it after the magical California in the book.

Later explorers discovered that this island wasn't an island at all, but a peninsula (now called Baja California)

connected to the mainland. The mainland (which became known as Alta California) was first explored by **Juan Rodriguez Cabrillo** in 1542. Everyone knew now that it wasn't an island, but the name California remained—some explorers were disappointed they didn't find the land filled with gold like the imaginary California in the book.

Before European contact, over 70 different Native American tribes lived in California. In 1769, Father **Junipero Serra**, a Spanish priest, began missionary work to these tribes,

Fr. Serra with Gaspar de Portola's expedition at San Diego, California in 1769

spreading the Gospel and founding missions all throughout the region. Before long, other missionaries and Spanish settlers followed him.

In 1821, when Mexico declared its independence from Spain, it took California with it. Then in 1846 California had its own revolution, and became the Republic of California—for only 22 days! At the same time, the Mexican-American War began and American troops quickly took over the new republic. When Mexico was defeated in 1848, the United States took formal possession of Alta California under the terms of the **Treaty of Guadalupe Hidalgo**; Mexico kept Baja California.

That year, there were fewer than 15,000 settlers in California. Then, something incredible happened. The same year California became a U.S. territory, a man named James Marshall found something completely unexpected in a stream at Sutter's Mill—gold!

Just like the imaginary land in the book, the real California truly was filled with gold! The next year, the

Gold miners in the Sierra Nevada Mountains

California Gold Rush began; thousands of "forty-niners" raced to California in search of the shiny nuggets. (Can you guess why they were called "forty-niners"?*)

By 1850, the population had skyrocketed and California became the 31st state. The Gold Rush didn't last long, but people are still drawn to "The Golden State"; today, more people live in California than in any other state. California has been strengthened and enriched by a diverse population, with about one-third claiming Hispanic heritage and one-tenth claiming Asian heritage. Immigrants from China arrived in the mid-1800s to work on the railroads; they were followed by Japanese immigrants and later, refugees from Vietnam fleeing from communism. More Native Americans live in California than in any other state.

*Answer: Because the Gold Rush began in 1849

Our third largest state has over 780 miles of mountainous Pacific coastline stretching from the Oregon border in the north down to the Mexican border in the south. The Cascade Mountains are in the north; the Sierra Nevada Mountains rise along the eastern border of the state. The word HUGE can't be used lightly about California—in this state you will find Mount Whitney, the tallest mountain in the contiguous United States; Lake Tahoe, which if drained could drown the entire state in over a foot of water; and California's giant redwoods, which are not only the world's biggest trees, but the biggest living things on earth!

Because of differences in climate, the cooler and wetter northern part of the state has a very different economy than the southern part of the state. Timber is a big part of the economy in Northern California. The forest products industry with its carefully managed forests allows timber to be cut and put to good use, while at the same time replanting and preserving forests for generations to come. (Similar practices are followed in all the western states, including Alaska, so that we will never run out of trees.)

In central California, south of the Cascade Mountains, lies the hot, fertile

A Giant Sequoia tree in winter

A Nation Built by Immigrants

Bishop Dominic Luong and the Lovers of the Holy Cross

In 1975, the government of Vietnam was taken over by communists. Life became very difficult under this government, particularly for people of faith. Thousands of Vietnamese fled and began new lives in America. Vietnamese-American immigrants and their children, many of them Catholics, now contribute to our society in many ways. Auxiliary Bishop Dominic Luong of Orange, California was named America's first Vietnamese-American bishop.

Our nation has also been enriched by a community of sisters that began more than 300 years ago in Vietnam, the Lovers of the Holy Cross. These sisters, "immigrants and descendants of immigrants," now serve the poor in California, too.

Central Valley, where California farmers grow over 200 different crops, providing about one-third of the country's food supply.

In the southeast you will find the fierce Mojave Desert. Death Valley earns its name by being the driest and hottest place in North America. Here you will also find the lowest point in the Western Hemisphere (282 feet below sea level). Amazingly, this spot is less than 90 miles from Mt. Whitney! The Colorado River forms the southeastern border of the state, and provides much-needed water to these desert places.

California lies along the Pacific's "***Ring of Fire***," an area of the world often hit by volcanic eruptions and earthquakes. Sometimes the earthquakes cause ***tsunamis***, or huge ocean waves that strike the coastlines. One such tsunami was caused by a severe Alaskan earthquake on Good Friday, 1964. The earthquake caused a tsunami that heavily damaged towns along the Alaskan coast and as far south as Crescent City, California!

California's economy is also diverse, which has made it one of the richest economies in the world. Since Steve Jobs and Stephen Wozniak started Apple Computer in a Cupertino garage in 1976, California has remained a leader in high-tech industries. The movie industry is centered in Los Angeles, yet not far from this huge city you will find miles and miles of farm and ranch land. California's warm weather is ideal for growing citrus fruits, grapes, and numerous vegetables that are found in grocery stores across the United States and beyond. Most of the walnuts, almonds, and plums found in our stores are grown here, and so much rice is grown in the Central Valley that it is ***exported***, or shipped out of the country, to Asia!

Tourists come to California to ride San Francisco's famous trolley cars and visit the Golden Gate Bridge. Millions of others each year visit magical natural attractions like Yosemite National Park and magical man-made attractions like Disneyland.

Yosemite National Park

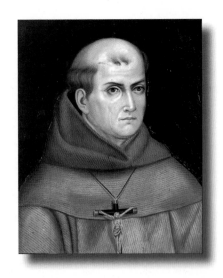

California's Catholic Heritage

The Story of St. Junipero Serra

In 1931, the people of California were asked to donate statues of two people from history to represent their state in the U.S. Capitol. Despite all the great men and women in California's dramatic history, one of the choices was made without hesitation—Father Junipero Serra. Father Serra had been an elderly priest, barely more than five feet tall, who somehow managed to look both frail and fat at the same time. He had very bad asthma and an even worse limp in his left leg. What a seemingly odd choice to represent the great state of California!

This unlikely hero of California was born Miguel Jose Serra on the Island of Majorca (off the coast of Spain) in 1713. Due to his tiny, weak body he was at first rejected for the priesthood, but eventually a group of Franciscans saw that his giant faith was more important than his small frame. So impressed were his superiors with his faith and intellect they appointed him a philosophy professor to train other priests—before he was even ordained himself!

It was in seminary that he took the name Junipero in honor of Brother Juniper,

St. Francis of Assisi's most faithful friend. Like Brother Juniper, Father Serra wanted to follow in the footsteps of the barefoot St. Francis—walking the world and spreading the Gospel to anyone he met. However, his superiors wanted him to stay home. They didn't believe his weak body could survive the trials of missionary work. Still, for years Father Serra prayed to be a missionary; when he was nearly 40 years old he finally found himself on a ship bound for Mexico. Yet again, his perseverance had paid off.

Not long after arriving in Mexico, Father Serra was stung by a scorpion on his left foot. The poison spread into his leg and practically paralyzed it. This injury caused him great pain for the rest of his life. Nevertheless, he always insisted on traveling by foot on his many long journeys. After all, isn't that what St. Francis had done centuries before?

For twenty years, Father Serra worked passionately among the Native Americans and Spanish settlers of Mexico. This alone would have been a great career for any missionary, but for Father Serra it was only the beginning. At that time, Russian ships were sighted sailing along the coast of Alta, or Upper, California. The Spanish were afraid that they would lose their claim to this land if they didn't settle it soon, so Father Serra eagerly suggested building a series of missions.

Three supply ships sailed on ahead but, as usual, Father Serra walked. The marching Spanish soldiers marveled at the elderly priest who insisted on limping alongside them. Then on July 16th, 1769, they reached their first destination, and the mission of San Diego was founded.

St. Junipero Serra, by N.C. Wyeth

Mission San Diego would be the first of nine missions Father Serra would personally found. Outside each he would hang a bell on the bough of a tree and ring it, inviting native people in. While he was eager to teach people about Jesus' love, Father Serra insisted on never forcing anyone to come against their will. Farming was virtually unknown to most of the tribes Father Serra encountered, so he also taught them how to raise crops so they would not have to rely on others for food.

When soldiers began abusing Native Americans, Father Serra traveled (on foot, of course) back to Mexico City with a list of laws designed to protect the rights and dignity of Native Americans.

Once again, Father Serra's perseverance paid off and the laws were approved.

When Father Serra was 71 years old, he became so ill that he couldn't leave his bed. A priest offered to bring him his final Communion, but Father Serra refused. "It is not for Our Lord to leave His place for me, but for me to go to Him." He limped to the chapel one last time.

All of the great cities of modern California grew from Serra's humble missions; the superhighways that connect these cities were first trod by this limping priest; the first seeds of this agricultural giant were sown by his little hands. Is anyone more deserving of the title, "Father of California"?

Hawaii

Honolulu

Ancient legends tell of a great sea-king called Hawai'i Loa, who paddled his canoe all around the Pacific in search of the perfect island. With only the stars as his guide, he finally found his paradise. He loved it so much he went home to bring his family to live there. When he brought them, more islands began to rise out of the sea—one for each of his many children. It's only a story, but legends often contain surprising truths.

Scientists now know that powerful volcanoes under the ocean violently erupted thousands of years ago. When the fiery lava cooled, it hardened and formed the **archipelago** (a string of islands) that now makes up the Hawaiian Islands. There was nothing magical about it, but in a way these islands did "rise out of the sea." Ancient people sometimes knew more than we give them credit for.

Ancient Polynesians first settled among the many islands of Hawaii over 2,000 years ago. Englishman **James Cook** was the first European to encounter the lands and its people in 1778. He named them the Sandwich Islands (after the Earl of Sandwich, who paid for Cook's explorations), but the name didn't stick. (Yes, sandwiches take their name from this Earl, who preferred to eat meat between two slices of bread. Another "mystery of history," solved.)

In 1810, **King Kamehameha I** united all the people of the many islands. The king was from the biggest island—Hawaii— and since then the entire group of islands have been known by this name.

After Cook's discovery, Hawaii became a convenient port in the Pacific for European sailors. As more Europeans came to Hawaii, the native people's way of life began to change. Christianity came to the Hawaiians, mostly through

Kee Beach, Kauai, Hawaii

Protestant missionaries. Unfortunately, many Hawaiians died from European diseases because they had no *immunity*, or natural ability to fight off these new illnesses. Over 20% of the population was wiped out by measles alone.

A trade agreement between Hawaii and the United States allowed American sugar plantation owners to gain a great deal of power in the islands. In 1893, these plantation owners overthrew Queen Lili'uokalani, the last queen of Hawaii. Despite protests from the Queen, from many Americans, and from even President Grover Cleveland, Hawaii was taken over by the United States in 1898 and became a U.S.

territory in 1900. Nearly a century later, the U.S. government apologized for the overthrow of the Hawaiian *monarchy*, the system by which Hawaii was ruled by kings and queens.

In 1941, a Japanese sneak attack on the Pearl Harbor naval base in Hawaii destroyed a number of ships and airplanes, and killed more than 2,300 people. This attack brought the United States into World War II. Thousands of people moved to Hawaii from the mainland to help with the war, fell in love with the islands, and never went back home. In 1959, Hawaii entered the Union as our youngest state.

Hawaii is the most southern state, the

Japanese Attack on Pearl Harbor, December 7, 1941, by Robert Grant Smith

Steam and spray mingle as active lava flows into the Pacific in Volcano National Park, Hawaii

only state completely surrounded by water, and the only state not part of the continent of North America. The Hawaiian Islands are separated from the continental United States by 2,400 miles of water! Would you like to visit this chain of tropical islands? Hawaii's tropical fruit is delicious and year-long sunny weather helps make tourism the main industry!

Now, which island would you like to visit? Although there are 132 islands throughout Hawaii, there are 8 main ones:

Farthest west is **Niihau**. Privately owned, "The Forbidden Isle" is generally off-limits to visitors; the owners have promised to preserve native Hawaiian culture here.

Next is **Kauai**, whose colorful rainforests give it the nickname "The Garden Isle." (Kauai's Mount Waialeale is the rainiest spot in the world!)

Most of Hawaii's population lives on **Oahu**, where you'll find Honolulu, the capital, and Waikiki—a beach of black volcanic sand where surfers speed down curling, 12-foot-high waves.

Next is **Molokai**, which you'll read about in the Catholic Heritage section.

The entire island of **Lanai** was once one big pineapple plantation!

No one lives on **Kahoolawe**, which is an enormous nature reserve, filled with beautiful tropical plants and wildlife.

Go whale-spotting in **Maui** before visiting **Hawaii**—"The Big Island." From a safe distance you can still watch active volcanoes erupt!

Hawaii has the greatest **ethnic**, or cultural and racial, diversity of any state; everyone belongs to a minority group! Barack Obama, our country's first African-American president, was born in Hawaii. The nation's first Chinese-American, Japanese-American, Thai-American congressmen, and the first Asian-American and Filipino-American governors were also all from Hawaii.

Today, native Hawaiians make up less than 1% of the population, but *leis* (garlands of flowers), *luaus* (traditional Hawaiian feasts) and the *hula* (a native dance) are known the world over.

A Nation Built by Immigrants

Daniel Inouye, World War II Hero and Senator

Hawaii is home to Americans whose ancestors immigrated from many Asian countries, including China, Korea, the Philippines, and Japan. One of the more famous Japanese-Americans was Hawaiian Senator Daniel Inouye. When

Pearl Harbor was attacked on Dec. 7th, 1941, seventeen-year-old Daniel hurried to help those wounded in the bombing. He later enlisted in the Army, and was himself seriously wounded in battle. For his brave actions, he was awarded the Medal of Honor. Later, when Hawaii became a state, Mr. Inouye became Hawaii's first representative in Congress. Two years after that, he was elected to the Senate, where he continued to represent Hawaii until his death at age 88. Senator Inouye served his country in wartime and peacetime for more than seventy years!

Hawaii's
Catholic Heritage

The Story of St. Damien

Jesus says, "Whatever you do to the least of your brothers, you do to Me." **Father Damien de Veuster** had these words in his heart when he volunteered in 1873 to live a life of isolation on the Hawaiian island of Molokai—the island of the lepers.

Leprosy (now called Hansen's disease) has struck fear in the hearts of mankind for thousands of years. In fact, we believe it is the world's oldest known disease. Victims of leprosy grow terrible sores on their skin. Nerve damage causes people to lose feeling in their fingers, hands, and legs, so they can suffer serious injuries without even knowing that they've hurt themselves. In time, repeated injuries can lead to the loss of these limbs.

In Biblical times, many people believed the horrible physical symptoms of leprosy meant that the person had committed an equally horrible, secret sin. As always, Jesus knew better. The stories of Jesus healing lepers are some of the most moving in the New Testament. However, 2,000 years later, some people with leprosy are still feared and shunned. In modern times, leprosy can be cured if treated early enough. Unfortunately, in some parts of the world many people

who get the disease do not seek medical help in time because they fear what others will think.

This dreaded disease started spreading among Hawaii's native people a few years before Father Damien arrived from his native Belgium. Since the Hawaiians had been separated from the rest of the world for so many centuries, they did not have the natural immunity needed to fight the disease. As leprosy spread rapidly through the islands, the King of Hawaii feared that soon all his people would be infected. His solution: send anyone showing signs of leprosy to the island of Molokai. There, these sick people would be isolated from the rest of the population.

The Molokai leper colony seemed the perfect solution, since it would stop the spread of the disease. But what about the lepers forced to live there? They had to stay on the island for the rest of their lives. No one could visit the island without risk of infection—without the risk of becoming "one of them"—the ugly, the sick, the disfigured, the unloved, and the unwanted. No one would dare—except Father Damien.

When Father Damien arrived, he was shocked by the smell of rotting flesh. He felt sick to his stomach at the sight of hundreds of people, so covered by open sores they barely seemed human. The situation was far worse than Father Damien imagined. He was sickened by the sight. How could he overcome this sickening feeling?

His solution: he started hugging the suffering lepers. He started hugging them and never stopped! This is the secret to sainthood. The saints are not perfect. Damien was as scared as you or I would be. Despite this, he touched the untouchable, and loved the unloved. That didn't make him perfect, but it did make him a saint.

For the rest of his life, Father Damien lived among the sick and the dying. His main goal was to return to them their dignity. He dressed their wounds with kindness. An avid athlete, Father Damien helped organize sporting events. His friends' physical disabilities never stood in the way. Some nights were filled with choir and band music: two former organ players had lost some of their fingers, but Father Damien showed them that between the two of them the church could ring with music again.

Father Damien's work soon gained international fame. Many respected what he was doing, but few were willing to follow him. One who did was Mother Marianne Cope from Illinois. She helped open a hospital on the island of Oahu, and took

a brief visit to Molokai where she was struck by the holiness of Father Damien.

Of all those who had poured praise on Father Damien, only one person came to his aid—Mother Marianne. Shortly after Mother Marianne's first visit, and after Fr. Damien had worked among the lepers for twelve years, he too was stricken by the feared disease. Mother Marianne nursed him through the last days of his life and promised to continue his work after his death. She kept this promise all the rest of her life—to touch the untouchable, to love the unloved.

Saint Damien was canonized in 2009, and Saint Marianne Cope in 2012.

Oregon

Salem

In 1543, the Spanish became the first Europeans to sight the Oregon coast. English sailor James Cook (remember him?) explored this coast over 200 years later.

Then, in 1805, Lewis and Clark travelled across Oregon to become the first explorers to cross the country all the way to the Pacific Ocean. In less than ten years, fur trading posts were set up in Oregon Country to buy furs from trappers and sell them overseas. The ***Hudson's Bay Company*** was one of these. Because it was a British company, Britain felt that it had a strong claim to Oregon Country (which also included what would become the state of Washington and part of Idaho).

By the 1840s, many American settlers were braving the 2,000 mile Oregon Trail from Independence, Missouri to settle and farm this frontier land. As more and more Americans entered Oregon, confusion over ownership of the territory almost led to war with Britain.

The Oregon Treaty of 1846 settled the issue peacefully, setting the present border between Washington State and Canada. Oregon then became a state in 1859.

The rocky mountains of the Coast Range run along the Pacific Ocean. East of the Coast Range, the Cascade Mountains also run north to south. Here you will

"Oregon Trail (Campfire)," by Albert Bierstadt

Hudson's Bay Company, "Shooting the Rapids," by Frances Anne Hopkins

find Mount Hood and Crater Lake—both were once lava-spewing volcanoes! In between these two ranges is the Willamette Valley, where most of the people live. The Columbia River forms most of the northern border of Oregon, and the Snake River forms more than half of the eastern border.

Oregon is the number one state in lumber production; huge forests of evergreens cover half the state. Oregon farms provide wheat and cattle, and factories produce computers and other electronics. If you visit Sea Lion Caves, you can't avoid the many cute creatures living there, but if you're not careful you might miss Mill Ends Park—the smallest park in the whole world!

Mill Ends Park, a two-foot-wide circle in Portland, Oregon

Did You Know? What Is a "Parallel"?

Have you been studying **longitude** and **latitude** in your Map Skills book? If so, you know that lines of longitude stretch up and down the globe, or map, from North Pole to South Pole. Lines of longitude mark distances from east to west.

Lines of latitude run parallel to the Equator, circling the globe like a belt circles your waist. Lines of latitude measure distances from north to south. The 49th Parallel runs east to west (or west to east!) and marks much of the border between the United States and Canada.

Washington

Olympia

Before Europeans explored the future state of Washington, Native American tribes flourished here. Then came the fur traders, and disagreements about who really owned this "Oregon Country."

The problem was settled with the Oregon Treaty of 1846, setting the border between Washington and Canada at the **49th Parallel**. In 1889, the people of this territory requested to become a state. The name suggested for the new state was "Columbia," but this name was rejected because it was felt people might confuse the state with Washington, D.C. (the District of Columbia).

Strangely, the "confusing" name was replaced with "Washington"! Our 42nd state is often referred to as Washington State to distinguish it from our nation's capital.

Mountains rise up along the Pacific coast of Washington. Perhaps the most famous of these is Mount St. Helens in the Cascade Mountains, which rained destruction when it erupted in 1980. To the east of these mountains lies the flat Columbia Plateau. The Columbia River flows through the southern part of the state and forms the Oregon border.

Mount St. Helens

Washington is famous for its apples, and grows more of this crop than any other place in the world. The Evergreen State also has a huge lumber industry. Wheat fields and cattle ranches are found in eastern Washington, but most of the population lives along the shores of Puget Sound to the west. Airplanes and aerospace equipment are built in Seattle, home of the 607-foot-high Space Needle. Totem poles stand proudly in the state's capital, reminders of the native peoples who still populate the state. (This tradition of carving totem poles continues today. Would you like to watch a totem pole being carved? Come to Washington!)

Space Needle

Did You Know?
What Is a Territory?

For thousands of years, countries around the world have claimed colonies, or territories. At one time, the Romans claimed the Holy Land, parts of Africa, and even England. Many Asian countries have "taken turns" ruling one another, depending on which country was the strongest at the time. Great Britain ruled colonies in Asia, South America, North America, Africa, and Australia. Spain held colonies in South America, Africa, and Asia. Oftentimes, the ruling country took more from the territory or colony than they gave back. At other times, the ruling country protected the colony or territory and helped it prosper.

You remember that, at our country's beginning, there were no states. Instead, there were thirteen colonies that were ruled by Great Britain. At the American Revolution, these thirteen colonies became one country with thirteen different states. Soon, new lands were added as territories, or lands that the U.S. Government controlled and protected. These territories were "ruled" by the U.S. Government, but were not yet states. In time, most of these territories became states.

In the last century or so, mostly because of wars, the United States has held territories outside our borders, too.

U.S. Territories

Did you know that the United States claims as U.S. territories 16 islands throughout the world? Most of these islands are *uninhabited*, or have no people living there, but the five largest have unique societies, and a unique relationship with the United States.

The tiny **Northern Mariana Islands,** far out in the Pacific, were placed under American protection after World War II. In the 1970s, the people who live on these islands voted not to seek independence as a separate country. Instead, they chose to become a U.S. territory. Most people here are Chamarros—people of mixed Indonesian, Spanish, and Filipino heritage.

The people of even tinier **American Samoa,** also in the Pacific Ocean, are mostly descendants of Polynesians who reached these islands thousands of years ago.

The Pacific island of **Guam** became a U.S. territory in 1898 following the Spanish-American War. Most land here is used by the U.S. military—members of the American military make up 20% of the population. This territory has a long Catholic heritage; Saint Pedro Calungsod was martyred in here in 1672.

In 1917, the United States purchased the **U.S. Virgin Islands** (in the Caribbean) from Denmark, whose colony it had been. Most of the people are descendants of slaves brought centuries ago by Europeans.

The largest and most populous U.S. territory is the Caribbean island of **Puerto Rico**. Claimed by Christopher Columbus in 1493 as a Spanish colony, the United States took control after the Spanish-American War. Some feel Puerto Rico should remain a U.S. territory and others think it should become an independent nation. Others feel it should take its place as the 51st state. What do you think will happen? Only time will tell . . .

Student Workbook: Complete pgs. 76-82.

The historic Castle San Felipe in San Juan, Puerto Rico

"The Gathering" by Sr. M. Julius Hausmann and Sr. M. Lurana Neely, courtesy of the Sisters of the Blessed Sacrament.
Photographed by Bob Borton/Fire and Ice Imagery.

Conclusion

You have learned that the United States of America was built by many peoples who came from all over the world, beginning with the arrival of native peoples 12,000 years ago, right up to the immigrants who arrive on our shores today. These diverse peoples chose to come to this great nation, to live united as one people: Americans. I hope the stories in this book show you how some Catholics have tried to make this nation a better place, from the beginning of American history to today.

You have learned of simple people who became great heroes, such as George Washington, Thomas Jefferson, and Charles Carroll, who fought for our country's independence, and also about those who wrote the law of our

203

land, the Constitution. Men like Father Sebastien Rale brought holiness into a new land others were only interested in conquering. Charles Carroll fought for American independence and religious freedom with words instead of guns. The Sweeds of Texas faced down racial prejudice, and Father Damien loved the unlovable. Women like Sister Blandina Segale brought Christ to Wild West outlaws, and men like Father Edward Flanagan brought our Heavenly Father to millions of orphans. Mother Angelica's dream of EWTN reaches millions more through radio, television, the internet, and beyond!

But what about you?

When Jesus rose from the dead on Easter Sunday the first person He revealed Himself to was Mary Magdalene. Why her? Why not Peter or one of the other Apostles? They were His chosen ones.

They would lead exciting lives of adventure in service of His Church. How small Mary Magdalene must have felt next to these great men. Yet when the time came to reveal His greatest miracle, Our Lord chose this humble woman with nothing but a simple prayer in her heart. God does everything for a wise and good reason.

I hope you enjoyed the stories of the great, Catholic, American heroes in this book. Their stories can inspire us, but remember there are millions of Catholics in this country trying to do God's will every day in their regular lives. They'll never be famous and no one will ever write a book about them. But God knows who they are.

You don't have to be famous to be a Catholic hero. Truly live the Faith of Jesus Christ and you can be a Catholic hero, too!

Turn to **LEARNING ABOUT MY STATE** on pg. 83 of your workbook to continue your study of the United States.

Special Thanks to:

Sister Angela (Angie) Gonzales, Holy Cross Parish, Santa Cruz, NM

Deacon Leonard Lockett, Vicar for Catholics of African Descent, Archdiocese of Galveston-Houston, TX

Theresa Nizza, Mission Nombre de Dios and Shrine of Our Lady of Leche, St. Augustine, FL

Works Cited

Addicks, Michael. "History of St. Mary Catholic Church - Brenham, Texas." *Polish Texans*. 12 July 2007. Web. <http://www.polish-texans.com/2007/07/history-of-st-mary-catholic-church-brenham-texas/>.

Allard, Paul. "Slavery and Christianity." *The Catholic Encyclopedia*. Vol. 14. New York: Robert Appleton, 1912. *New Advent*. Web. <http://www.newadvent.org/cathen/14036a.htm>.

Allen, John L., Jr. "Texas: New Catholic Frontier." *National Catholic Reporter* 18 Apr. 2008, A. Cover sec. Web. <http://ncronline.org/node/699>.

"Archbishop Charles J. Seghers." *Archdiocese of Portland in Oregon*. Web. <http://www.archdpdx.org/previous-abs/bios/ab_seghers.htm>.

Arroyo, Raymond. *Mother Angelica: The Remarkable Story of a Nun, Her Nerve, and a Network of Miracles*. New York: Doubleday, 2005. Print.

Bennett, Mark. "In Rome, Indiana Pilgrims Gather at Vigil on Eve of Canonization." *Tribune-Star* [Terre Haute, IN] 15 Oct. 2006. Web. <http://www.news-tribune.net/religion/local_story_288123442.htm>.

Birdsall, Stephen S., and John W. Florin. *Outline of American Geography: Regional Landscapes of the United States*. Washington, D.C.: United States Information Agency, 1998. *U.S. Diplomatic Mission to Germany*. Web. <http://usa.usembassy.de/etexts/outgeogr/homepage.htm>.

"Bl. Marianne Cope (1838-1918)." *The Vatican*. Web. <http://www.vatican.va/news_services/liturgy/saints/ns_lit_doc_20050514_molokai_en.html>.

"Blessed Damien Bio." *Congregation of the Sacred Hearts of Jesus and Mary: United States Province*. Web. <http://www.sscc.org/pages/x_Damien/damien_bio.htm>.

Blessed Virgin Mary Catholic Church, Washington, Texas. Web. <http://home.catholicweb.com/Blessed_Virgin_Mary_Catholic_Church/index.cfm>.

Bockenhauer, Mark H., and Stephen F. Cunha. *Our Fifty States*. Washington, D.C.: National Geographic Society, 2004. Print.

Boeynaems, Libert. "Father Damien (Joseph De Veuster)." *The Catholic Encyclopedia*. Vol. 4. New York: Robert Appleton, 1908. *New Advent*. Web. <http://www.newadvent.org/cathen/04615a.htm>.

Boyer, Paul S. "The Middle West." *The Oxford Companion to United States History*. 2001. *Encyclopedia.com*. Web. <http://www.encyclopedia.com>.

Boys Town. Web. <http://www.boystown.org/>.

Butler, Alban, and Michael J. Walsh. *Butler's Lives of the Saints*. San Francisco: Harper & Row, 1985. Print.

Carroll, Anne W. *Christ and the Americas*. Rockford, IL: Tan, 1997. Print.

"Catholic Diocese of Fairbanks Overview." *Catholic Diocese of Fairbanks*. Web. <http://dioceseoffairbanks.org/diocesanoverview/index.shtml>.

Cheney, Lynne V., and Robin Preiss-Glasser. *Our 50 States: A Family Adventure across America*. New York: Simon & Schuster for Young Readers, 2006. Print.

Christian, Carole E. "Brenham, TX." *Handbook of Texas Online*. Texas State Historical Association. Web. <http://www.tshaonline.org/handbook/online/articles/heb11>.

"Church Matriarch Dies at 102." *KXAN TV*. 3 Nov. 2011. Web. <http://www.kxan.com/dpp/news/local/church-matriarch-dies-at-102>.

Clarita, Sister M. *Leaders of Freedom*. Long Prairie, MN: Neumann, 1997. Print.

Connor, Rev. Charles P. *Our American Catholic Heritage*. CTV. Scranton, PA, 1995. Television.

Corley, John. "Missouri." *The Catholic Encyclopedia*. Vol. 10. New York: Robert Appleton, 1911. *New Advent*. Web. <http://www.newadvent.org/cathen/10398a.htm>.

Cowan, Thomas Dale. *The Way of the Saints: Prayers, Practices, and Meditations*. New York: Putnam, 1998. Print.

Cox, Patrick J. "The Ecclesiology of Las Posadas." Thesis. St. Norbert College, De Pere, WI, 2007. Print.

Crimont, Joseph. "Alaska." *The Catholic Encyclopedia*. Vol. 1. New York: Robert Appleton, 1907. *New Advent*. Web. <http://www.newadvent.org/cathen/01246b.htm>.

Deasy, John. "Ohio." *The Catholic Encyclopedia*. Vol. 11. New York: Robert Appleton, 1911. *New Advent*. Web. <http://www.newadvent.org/cathen/11225d.htm>.

Donlon, J.P. "Best / Worst States for Business 2011." *Chief Executive*. 3 May 2011. Web. <http://chiefexecutive.net/best-worst-states-for-business>.

Donovan, Sandra. *The Hispanic American Experience*. Minneapolis: Twenty-First Century, 2011. Print.

Elson, John, and Richard N. Ostling. "Mother Knows Best." *Time* 7 Aug. 1995. Web. <http://www.time.com/time/magazine/article/0,9171,983275,00.html>.

Engelhardt, Zephyrin. "California Missions." *The Catholic Encyclopedia*. Vol. 3. 1908. *New Advent*. Web. <http://www.newadvent.org/cathen/03177b.htm>.

Engelhardt, Zephyrin. "Junípero Serra." *The Catholic Encyclopedia*. Vol. 13. New York: Robert Appleton, 1912. *New Advent*. Web. <http://www.newadvent.org/cathen/13730b.htm>.

Evans, Roxanne J. "Black Catholics." *Handbook of Texas Online*. Texas State Historical Association. Web. <http://www.tshaonline.org/handbook/online/articles/icb03>.

EWTN Global Catholic Television Network. Web. <http://www.ewtn.com/>.

Fanning, William. "Pierre-Jean De Smet." *The Catholic Encyclopedia*. Vol. 4. New York: Robert Appleton, 1908. *New Advent*. Web. <http://www.newadvent.org/cathen/04752a.htm>.

"Father Flanagan Biography." *Father Flanagan League Society of Devotion*. Web. <http://fatherflanagan.org/biography.php>.

"Father McGivney." *Knights of Columbus Rev. James P. Heede Council #7246*. Web. <http://www.newportnet.com/kc7246/McGivney.html>.

Fialka, John J. *Sisters: Catholic Nuns and the Making of America*. New York: St. Martin's, 2003. Print.

"Francis J. Parater, Servant of God." *The Catholic Diocese of Richmond*. Web. <http://www2.richmonddiocese.org/parater/>.

Furlong, Most Rev. Philip Joseph, and Helen M. Ganey. *Our Pioneers and Patriots*. Rockford, IL: Tan, 1997. Print.

Ghezzi, Bert. *Voices of the Saints: A Year of Readings*. New York: Image, 2002. Print.

Gonzales, Sr. Angela. "The Journey of Mary and Joseph - Las Posadas." Letter to the author. 18 May 2012. MS. Santa Cruz, New Mexico.

Gordon, Patricia, and Reed C. Snow. *Kids Learn America! Bringing Geography to Life with People, Places, and History*. Charlotte, VT.: Williamson, 1999. Print.

Haddad, Lester Mark. "Maryland." *In God We Trust: Our Christian Heritage*. Savannah, GA: Cross Publications, 2012. *Mary Your Mother*. Web. <http://www.maryourmother.net/Maryland.html>.

Harrington, Thomas. "Massachusetts." *The Catholic Encyclopedia*. Vol. 10. New York: Robert Appleton, 1911. *New Advent*. Web. <http://www.newadvent.org/cathen/10024c.htm>.

"Hawaiian Historical Legends: A Viking of the Pacific." *Internet Sacred Text Archive*. Web. <http://www.sacred-texts.com/pac/hhl/hhl08.htm>.

Hearn, Edward. "Knights of Columbus." *The Catholic Encyclopedia*. Vol. 8. New York: Robert Appleton, 1911. *New Advent*. Web. <http://www.newadvent.org/cathen/08670c.htm>.

Hill, Genny. "A Personal Reflection: Parish Matriarch Inspired Generations of Catholics." *Catholic Spirit* Jan. 2012. Diocese of Austin. Web. <http://www.austindiocese.org/newsletter_article_view.php?id=6447>.

Horvat, Marian T. "The Burning of the Ursuline Convent in Charlestown." *Tradition in Action*. 28 Jan. 2011. Web. <http://www.traditioninaction.org/History/B_018_UrsulineConvent_1.html>.

Horvat, Marian T. "Let None Dare Call It Liberty: The Catholic Church in Colonial America." *Tradition in Action*. Web. <http://www.traditioninaction.org/History/B_001_Colonies.html>.

Horvat, Marian T. "St. Philippine Duchesne: Failures Became Her Success." *Tradition in Action*. Web. <http://www.traditioninaction.org/religious/c006rpPhillipineDuschene.shtml>.

"Jacques Marquette Biography." *Visitors Guide to the Middle Mississippi River Valley*. Web. <http://www.greatriverroad.com/pere/marquettebio.htm>.

January, Brendan. *The Thirteen Colonies*. New York: Children's, 2000. Print.

Keenan, Sheila, and Selina Alko. *Greetings from the 50 States: How They Got Their Names*. New York: Scholastic, 2008. Print.

Ketcham, William. "Bureau of Catholic Indian Missions." *The Catholic Encyclopedia*. Vol. 7. New York: Robert Appleton, 1907. *New Advent*. Web. <http://www.newadvent.org/cathen/07745a.htm>.

Knott, Aloysius. "Maryland." *The Catholic Encyclopedia*. Vol. 9. New York: Robert Appleton, 1910. *New Advent*. Web. <http://www.newadvent.org/cathen/09755b.htm>.

Krauthamer, Barbara. "Slavery." *Encyclopedia of Oklahoma History & Culture*. Oklahoma Historical Society. Web. <http://digital.library.okstate.edu/encyclopedia/entries/S/SL003.html>.

Lockett, Dn. Leonard. "Re: Catholic Geography Textbook." Message to the author. 3 Aug. 2012. E-mail.

Lockett, Dn. Leonard. "Re: Catholic Geography Textbook." Message to the author. 4 Aug. 2012. E-mail.

Lockett, Dn. Leonard. Telephone interview. 3 Aug. 2012.

Loughlin, James. "Archdiocese of Philadelphia." *The Catholic Encyclopedia*. Vol. 11. New York: Robert Appleton, 1911. *New Advent*. Web. <http://www.newadvent.org/cathen/11793b.htm>.

Lowth, Catherine. "Philippine-Rose Duchesne." *The Catholic Encyclopedia*. Vol. 5. New York: Robert Appleton, 1909. *New Advent*. Web. <http://www.newadvent.org/cathen/05182a.htm>.

Lukes, Bonnie L. *Colonial America*. San Diego, CA: Lucent, 2000. Print.

Manser, Martin H., and David Pickering. *Dictionary of Saints*. London: Collins, 2004. Print.

McQueen, Clyde. *Black Churches in Texas: A Guide to Historic Congregations.* College Station: Texas A & M UP, 2000. Print.

Meehan, Thomas. "Boston." *The Catholic Encyclopedia.* Vol. 2. New York: Robert Appleton, 1907. *New Advent.* Web. <http://www.newadvent.org/cathen/02703a.htm>.

"Midwest." *The Columbia Encyclopedia.* 6th ed. 2008. *Encyclopedia.com.* Web. <http://www.encyclopedia.com>.

"Midwest." *Dictionary of American History.* 2003. *Encyclopedia. com.* Web. <http://www.encyclopedia.com>.

Mission of Nombre De Dios and Shrine of Our Lady of La Leche. Web. <http://www.missionandshrine.org/>.

Monuments and Historic Places of America. New York: Macmillan Library Reference USA, 2000. Print.

Mooney, Joseph. "Archdiocese of New York." *The Catholic Encyclopedia.* Vol. 11. New York: Robert Appleton, 1911. *New Advent.* Web. <http://www.newadvent.org/cathen/11020a.htm>.

Morice, Adrian. "Charles John Seghers." *The Catholic Encyclopedia.* Vol. 13. New York: Robert Appleton, 1912. *New Advent.* Web. <a. http://www.newadvent.org/cathen/13682a.htm>.

"Mother Angelica." *Shrine of the Most Blessed Sacrament.* Web. <http://www.olamshrine.com/Mother.htm>.

Nevins, Albert J. . *Builders of Catholic America.* Huntington, IN: Our Sunday Visitor, 1985. Print.

Nevins, Albert J. *American Martyrs: From 1542.* Huntington, IN: Our Sunday Visitor Pub. Division, Our Sunday Visitor, 1987. Print.

Nevins, Albert J. *Our American Catholic Heritage.* Huntington, IN: Our Sunday Visitor, 1972. Print.

Nizza, Theresa. Telephone interview. 19 Feb. 2012.

O'Brien, Matthew. "Cincinnati." *The Catholic Encyclopedia.* Vol. 3. New York: Robert Appleton, 1908. *New Advent.* Web. <http://www.newadvent.org/cathen/03773a.htm>.

Ochoa, George. *Atlas of Hispanic-American History.* New York: Facts on File, 2001. Print.

Owens, Reginald. "The Forgotten Story." Feb. 2002. Web. <http://www.tpwmagazine.com/archive/2002/feb/ed_4/>.

"Region Description: Mid-Atlantic." *National Gardening Association.* 2012. Web. <http://www.garden.org/regional/report/description/full/13>.

"The Regions of the United States." *U.S. Diplomatic Mission to Germany.* Web. <http://usa.usembassy.de/travel-regions.htm>.

"Saint Mother Theodore." *Sisters of Providence of Saint-Mary-of-the-Woods.* Web. <http://www.spsmw.org/sisters-of-providence/saint-mother-theodore.aspx>.

Schuyler, Henry. "Sebastian Râle (Rasle)." *The Catholic Encyclopedia.* Vol. 12. New York: Robert Appleton, 1911. *New Advent.* Web. <http://www.newadvent.org/cathen/12635b.htm>.

Segale, Sr. Blandina, and Therese Martin. *At the End of the Santa Fe Trail.* Milwaukee: Bruce, 1948. Print.

"Servant of God Frank Parater." *Catholic Diocese of Arlington.* 7 Feb. 2002. Web. <http://www.arlingtondiocese.org/vocations/voc_parater.php>.

Shapiro, William E., ed. *The Student Encyclopedia of the United States.* Boston: Kingfisher, 2005. Print.

Sirvaitis, Karen. *The European American Experience.* Minneapolis: Twenty-First Century, 2011. Print.

"The South." *Columbia Encyclopedia.* 6th ed. 2008. *Encyclopedia.com.* Web. <http://www.encyclopedia.com>.

Spalding, Henry. "Jacques Marquette, S.J." *The Catholic Encyclopedia.* Vol. 9. New York: Robert Appleton, 1910. *New Advent.* Web. <http://www.newadvent.org/cathen/09690a.htm>.

Sr. Jeanne Marie. "Frontier Missionary of the Sacred Heart: Saint Rose Philippine Duchesne (1769-1852)." *Catholicism.org.* Slaves of the Immaculate Heart of Mary, 6 Mar. 2009. Web. <http://catholicism.org/saint-rose-philippine-duchesne.html>.

Sr. M. Augusta. *Guardian of Freedom.* Long Prairie, MN: Neumann, 1997. Print.

Sr. M. Theresine. *Challenge of Freedom.* Long Prairie, MN: Neumann, 1997. Print.

Sr. M. Veronica. *Bearers of Freedom.* Long Prairie, MN: Neumann, 1997. Print.

Sr. Mercedes. "Sisters of the Blessed Sacrament." *The Catholic Encyclopedia.* Vol. 2. New York: Robert Appleton, 1907. *New Advent.* Web. <http://www.newadvent.org/cathen/02599a.htm>.

"St. Theodore Guerin Biography - The Legacy." *Guerin Catholic High School.* Web. <http://www.guerincatholic.org/p_about/biography.php>.

Stace, Francis. "Michigan." *The Catholic Encyclopedia.* Vol. 10. New York: Robert Appleton, 1911. *New Advent.* Web. <http://www.newadvent.org/cathen/10280a.htm>.

Steckler, Gerard G. "Seghers, Charles John (Charles-Jean, Karl Jan)." *Dictionary of Canadian Biography Online.* 2000. Web. <http://www.biographi.ca/009004-119.01-e.php>.

Stein, Mark. *How the States Got Their Shapes.* New York: Smithsonian /Collins, 2008. Print.

"Texas Independence Trail Region." *African-Americans in Texas: A Lasting Legacy.* Texas Historical Commission, 2012. Web. <http://www.africanamericansintexas.com/regions/texas-independence-trail-region>.

"Theodore Guerin (1798-1856)." *The Vatican.* Web. <http://www.vatican.va/news_services/liturgy/saints/ns_lit_doc_20061015_guerin_en.html>.

"US Seminarian Is Headed for Sainthood." *Xavierian Mission Newsletter* (15 Feb. 2002). *Xavierian Missionaries USA.* Web. <http://www.xaviermissionaries.org/M_Life/NL_Archives/2002-N_Lett/US_Parater1.htm>.

Veale, James. "Florida." *The Catholic Encyclopedia*. Vol. 6. New York: Robert Appleton, 1909. *New Advent*. Web. <http://www.newadvent.org/cathen/06115b.htm>.

Venerable Michael J. McGivney. Web. <http://www.fathermcgivney.org/en/index.html>.

Villarreal, Sylvia. "Washington County Home to State's Oldest African American Catholic Church." *KBTX*. 23 Feb. 2009. Web. <http://www.kbtx.com/home/headlines/40202012.html>.

Webb, Marcus. *The United States*. San Diego, CA: Lucent, 2000. Print.

Wexler, Sanford, ed. *Westward Expansion: An Eyewitness History*. New York: Facts on File, 1991. Print.

Wright, Robert E., O.M.I. "Catholic Church." *Handbook of Texas Online*. Texas State Historical Association. Web. <http://www.tshaonline.org/handbook/online/articles/icc01>.

Zehnder, Christopher. *From Sea to Shining Sea: The Story of America*. San Francisco: Ignatius, 2003. Print.

Image Credits

Special Thanks to:

Cover and pgs. i, 56, 203: "The Gathering" by Sr. M. Julius Hausmann and Sr. M. Lurana Neely, photographed by Bob Borton/Fire and Ice Imagery and provided courtesy of the Archives of the Sisters of the Blessed Sacrament. The mural hangs in the Motherhouse of the Sisters in Bensalem, PA.

Pg. 56: Photo of St. Katharine Drexel provided courtesy of the Archives of the Sisters of the Blessed Sacrament.

Pg. 22: Courtesy of the Knights of Columbus.

Pg. 23: Painting by Antonella Cappuccio, Oil on canvas 2003. Courtesy of the Knights of Columbus.

Pg. 28: Public domain, photo courtesy of Fr. Vincent Lapomarda.

Pg. 48: Public domain, courtesy of Corpus Christi Watershed.

Pg. 49: Courtesy of the Missionary Sisters of the Sacred Heart of Jesus, Radnor, PA.

Pg. 49: Public domain, courtesy of www.famvin.org.

Pg. 55: Mosaic located at The Shrine of St. John Neumann in Philadelphia, PA. Photo reprinted with permission of the Redemptorists of the Baltimore Province, 2012.

Pg. 66: Courtesy of the Sisters of Providence of Saint Mary-of-the-Woods, Indiana, Inc.

Pg. 78: Courtesy of the Archdiocese of Louisville, KY.

Pg. 88: Courtesy of Villa Duchesne and Oak Hill School, St. Louis, Missouri

Pg. 120: Painting by Anne Chapin, located in the North American College in Rome, Italy. Courtesy of the Catholic Diocese of Richmond.

Pg. 121: Courtesy of the Catholic Diocese of Richmond.

Pg. 136: Courtesy of EWTN.

Pgs. 142, 145: © City of St. Martinville, LA. Funded by individual donations/memorials and by the National Endowment for the Arts, the Louisiana State Arts Council, and the Louisiana Division of the Arts, and the Office of the Cultural Development in the Department of Culture, Recreation, and Tourism, and the Acadiana Arts Council.

Pg. 151: Blessed Virgin Mary Catholic Church, Washington, TX, via http://home.catholicweb.com/Blessed_Virgin_Mary_Catholic_Church/

Pg. 161, 162: Courtesy of the Sisters of Charity, Cincinnati, http://srcharitycinti.org

Pg. 175: Courtesy Julie Libersat. © Julie Libersat/Times Illustrated.

Pg. 185: Photos of Sacred Heart Cathedral, Fairbanks, AK, via www.cbna.info/parishprofiles/fairbankssacredheartcathedral.shtml

Pg. 190: Public domain, courtesy of Mission San Juan Capistrano, CA

Pgs. 196, 197: Courtesy of the Archives of the Congregation of the Sacred Hearts in Rome (SS.CC. ARCHIVES, ROME)

Credits:

126: The Wright Brothers, Tacconi, Ferdinando (1922-2006)/Private Collection/© Look and Learn; pgs. 157, 159: Seeking the New Home (oil on canvas), Wyeth, Newell Convers (1882-1945)/Private Collection/Photo © Christie's Images.

Thinkstock.com: miniature "mysteries of history" magnifying glass, pgs. 21, 30, 34, 41, 47, 59, 77, 80, 84, 116, 128, 166: Hemera; cover and pg. i: iStockphoto; pg. vi: Stockbyte/Stockbyte; pg. 87: iStockphoto; pg. 100: iStockphoto; pg. 100: iStockphoto; pg. 113: iStockphoto; pg. 123: iStockphoto; pg. 123: Hemera; pg. 132, 133: iStockphoto; pg. 139: iStockphoto; pg. 166: iStockphoto; pg. 202: Comstock/Comstock.

Via Wikimedia Commons:

Public Domain, {{PD-US}}: front and back covers and pgs. i, i, iv, iv, v, v, vi, 3, 4, 5, 6, 7, 9, 15, 17, 20, 20, 24, 24, 25, 30, 31, 32, 33, 34, 35, 42, 43, 44, 50, 51, 52, 53, 53, 53, 57, 63, 63, 63, 64, 69, 71, 72, 73, 74, 75, 76, 76, 77, 81, 82, 83, 84, 87, 90, 92, 95, 99, 99, 103, 105, 105, 111, 112, 114, 116, 116, 117, 118, 118, 124, 129, 130, 132, 132, 133, 139, 140, 141, 142, 153, 155, 157, 158, 159, 160, 163, 180, 180, 181, 187, 198, 199, 200.

CC-BY-SA-2.5 (http://creativecommons.org/licenses/by-sa/2.5): pgs. 97, 147.

CC-BY-SA-3.0 (http://creativecommons.org/licenses/by-sa/3.0/): pgs. 81, 100, 133, 169, 201.

CC-BY-2.0 (http://creativecommons.org/licenses/by/2.0): pgs. 164, 167, 199.

pg. 43, 52: Serguey - Own work, CC BY 3.0, (https://commons.wikimedia.org/w/index.php?curid=2747292)

pg. 74: Heironymous Rowe CC BY-SA 3.0 via (https://commons.wikimedia.org/wiki/File:Serpent_Mound1_HRoe_2005.jpg#/media/File:Serpent_Mound1_HRoe_2005.jpg)

pg. 194 - Own work, CC BY-SA 3.0, (https://commons.wikimedia.org/w/index.php?curid=6487450)

Encore-Editions.com: pgs. 8, 17, 40, 144, 157, 173, 191